THE
IRISH ROOTS
GUIDE

Tony McCarthy

D0048236

THE LILLIPUT PRESS

First published in 1991 by
THE LILLIPUT PRESS LTD
4 Rosemount Terrace, Arbour Hill,
Dublin 7, Ireland

A CIP record for this
title is available from
The British Library.

ISBN 0 946640 77 7

Set and formatted in 10 on 11 Palatino
on an Apple Macintosh II si (*Quark Xpress*)
and printed in Dublin by
Colour Books of Baldoyle

CONTENTS

ILLUSTRATIONS

PREFACE AND ACKNOWLEDGMENTS

When your ancestors are Irish, 'doing your family tree' can be difficult, time-consuming and costly. This book provides all the guidance necessary to accomplish the task; it helps you to make optimum use of your time and keep expenses to the minimum. It should be read through and then used for reference.

A number of people have assisted me in the production of *The Irish Roots Guide*. Mr Maurice Thuillier and Mr Sean Lydon read an early draft and offered some useful suggestions. Mr Tim Cadogan of the Cork County Library and Mr Kieran Burke of the Cork City Library were most helpful when I was researching various genealogical sources. I spent a great deal of time in Irish archives. Knowledgeable and obliging staff made my task easier than I had imagined. To all those I wish to express my thanks.

It is impossible to write a book like this without a degree of plagiarism. I have tried to include in the 'Bibliography and Sources' all the works I have used.

I would like to thank the Deputy Keeper of the Records, Public Record Office of Northern Ireland for permission to quote from the Earl of Listowel's papers; and the editor of the *Journal of the Cork Historical and Archaeological Society* for permission to quote from an article by Mr R. Henchion.

Finally, I would like to thank my wife, Angela, without whose help this book would not have been written.

FOREWORD

The search for family roots is no longer the exclusive activity of North Americans and Australians interested in their Irish forebears. At home, more and more Irish people are anxious to trace their ancestry.

Today, amateur genealogists are facilitated by the availability of well-organized records but they are also frustrated by a lack of any clear idea of where to begin their investigation, and how to continue their labour of love.

Such people – the great majority of family researchers – will find Tony McCarthy's book an invaluable guide. Indeed, the author can fully stand over his claim that his work is 'the most complete guide available to the twelve best sources of genealogical information'.

He suggests a novel approach to 'doing the family tree', reminding us to cherish all our ancestors equally, not just in the male 'mainline'. His very readable book combines learning and usefulness with common sense and humour, as he gently warns us of frequent errors and pitfalls.

Finally, it is worth noting that the work has the seal of academic approval. For his independent research, the author has been awarded an honours MA degree by the National University of Ireland.

JOHN A. MURPHY
Emeritus Professor of Irish History
University College Cork

1

INTRODUCTION

About ten years ago I started to research the history of my own family. As soon as I began to accumulate information, I found it necessary to clarify my objectives because I felt dissatisfied with the family tree that I found myself constructing. I had begun by concentrating exclusively on the male line; my purpose being to trace it back as far as possible. This is the traditional procedure, employed in the most readily available guidebooks. Popular literature on the subject also encourages the reader to equip himself with a *history of his surname* and the family *coat of arms*.

I am unhappy with this procedure for many reasons. It consigns the greater part of one's ancestry to oblivion, while attaching exaggerated importance to those who bore one's surname. The notion that a surname is but a means of identification, a tag or label, would be strongly contested by some, but it would be foolish to maintain that its significance is on a par with the most important thing conveyed to us by our ancestors – life. In this respect it is undeniable that the role of each one of our ancestors was crucial and equal.

MALE LINE

How then has what might be termed 'mainline genealogy' triumphed over invincible biological fact? A widespread misunderstanding of Burke's and Debrett's publications is, I suspect, one of the main reasons. *Burke's Peerage, Burke's Landed Gentry* and similar genealogical works very deliberately concentrate on the male line, to the extent of listing children, not strictly in order of birth, but boys first, followed by girls. In the introduction to *Burke's Irish Family Records*, the reason given for this procedure is 'primogeniture', the right of succession belonging to the first-born male, or to the eldest surviving male. The principal purpose of Burke's and similar family trees is not, as is widely believed, to give a comprehensive account of the

1

ancestry of those listed. It is to illustrate how title and property descended through various generations. A family tree of this type is like a map showing the route taken by title and property from times past to the present. It is quite legitimate and understandable for anybody who has inherited property, be it ever so humble, to wish to trace the inheritance back through the generations; and as all property descends in the same way, he will find himself concentrating on his male line. However, I suspect that most people who trace their family trees are, like myself, descended from the non-propertied majority. In that case to concentrate on the male line is to follow uncritically Burke's and Debrett's model.

The domination of the male line over the female line in genealogy is consistent with male domination, up to recent times at least, in almost all spheres. Once, women were virtually regarded as mere incubators, within whom the male seed grew to viable proportions. Science has shown that men and women are equal partners in the process of procreation. Children in secondary school learn in biology class that chromosomes are the genetic building-blocks; that 23 chromosomes are provided by the male sperm and an equal number by the female ovum. However, genealogy, by its insistence on the exclusive importance of the male line, still proceeds according to the primitive perception of women. It must only be a matter of time before this gross example of male chauvinism is swept away by liberated women tracing their foremothers. Indeed, it has become fashionable for women to retain their own surnames after marriage and even to impose double-barrelled names on their offspring. Should this tendency persist over a number of generations, a surname could become a veritable genealogical table.

SURNAME

Quite often, little may be unearthed about individuals who lived in past centuries, apart from Christian name, surname and the townland in which they lived. A common surname helps people to identify with their ancestors. This is another reason why family historians have tended to deal with the main line only. People don't feel comfortable with a list of ancestors

whose surnames differ from their own. They are like strangers.
Studying the history of one's surname leads to a stronger
identification, an emotional bonding with it. One begins to
regard oneself as a Sullivan or a Kelly. A feeling akin to nation-
alism develops. The notion of belonging to a particular clan or
sept is popular in Ireland and even more popular in the United
States. Such notions do not stand up to analysis, however. Our
parents have two surnames, our grandparents four. Stretching
back another generation, our great-grandparents have eight
surnames. If social convention did not eliminate seven of these,
the clan fantasy would not exist. One cannot belong
simultaneously to eight clans.

COAT OF ARMS

Buying the coat of arms associated with one's surname com-
pletes the process of identification with a small segment of one's
ancestry. Such a purchase is doubly foolish. First, it shuts out
from one's consideration the vast majority of those to whom
one owes one's existence. Second, the belief that every surname
has its corresponding coat of arms is incorrect. Commercial
interests have sought to increase their market by promoting the
idea that, just as every birthday has its star sign, every surname
has its coat of arms. This is not true. Coats of arms belong to
particular families and not to all those who bear a common
surname. They may be seen in the same way as hereditary titles.
If your name happens to be Gerald Grosvenor, it does not mean
that you may call yourself the Duke of Westminster. Only the
families to whom the hereditary title or coat of arms belong
may use them. One authoritative writer on heraldry makes the
point that those who purport to sell representations of a
person's arms, simply on the evidence of his surname, may be
open to legal action by the purchaser, since the vendor is
describing his wares incorrectly and making money by false
pretences.

To be entitled to use a coat of arms in Ireland, it is necessary
to show unbroken male descent from some person to whom
arms were granted by patent and officially registered either in
the Genealogical Office or in its predecessor, Ulster's Office of
Arms. An alternative method is to prove that a particular coat

of arms was in use by your family for a hundred years and three generations.

The idea of sept arms is partly to blame for the general confusion concerning coats of arms in Ireland. It seems to have been accepted at one time that proof of sept membership entitled one to use the arms of the sept. The acceptance of the principle of sept arms, however, never implied that arms appertained to surnames. A sept is a collective term describing a group of people who not only bore a common surname but also inhabited a particular area or whose ancestors are known to have inhabited that area.

There are several distinct septs of O'Kelly, for example. The O'Kellys of Meath would have had no more right to the arms of the O'Kellys of Ui Maine than a Murphy or an O'Sullivan. Officially no one is entitled to use sept arms except the chief of the name.

NEW APPROACH

Having rejected the traditional approach to 'doing the family tree', I could see no logical alternative apart from researching all my ancestral lines. On the face of it, this seems like a daunting task, especially when we consider that the number of our ancestors per generation doubles with each step we take backwards in time. We have two parents; six steps further back, we have 128 great, great, great, great, great, grandparents; three additional steps and the number is over 1000. Go back to the twentieth generation and the number of ancestors tops the million – quite the reverse of the expectations of ancient genealogists, who thought they were tracing families back to two individuals, Adam and Eve, and indeed often claimed to have done so. The million ancestors, of course, is a theoretical number. It is based on the false premise that our ancestors were related to one another in no way but the obvious. When first cousins marry, their children have six and not eight great-grandparents. Family trees are full of such interconnections. In any case, Irish records are so bad that one is lucky if all one's ancestral lines do not disappear around the fifth or sixth generation.

GUIDEBOOKS

At this point, having clarified my objectives, I began to think of how to attain them. I found that there are several publications available which claim to guide those wishing to research their family history. They range from Margaret Dickson Falley's weighty two-volume work, *Irish and Scotch-Irish Ancestral Research*, through the shorter *Handbook on Irish Genealogy* by the Heraldic Artists, down to a variety of cheap pamphlets. Although I learned a great deal from these publications, I didn't find any one book to be completely satisfactory.

Their chief defect is that they try to be too comprehensive: to offer guidance to everybody with Irish roots. The fact that ancestors must be looked at in the context of their social position is largely ignored. This is a crucial mistake because a person's class had a great bearing on whether or not he figured in particular types of records. Few will consult a Church of Ireland register in search of a Catholic baptismal entry (although in some Donegal and the midlands registers, many such entries are to be found). Searching the Registry of Deeds for a small tenant farmer's lease is almost as fruitless an occupation as searching nineteenth-century newspapers for a cottier's death notice.

A second defect is the lack of suitably detailed information about the documents which form the source material for ancestral research. It comes as a surprise to the beginner when he discovers that the entries in many Catholic registers are written in Latin, in bad handwriting and on paper spotty with decay. Novices are inclined to accept as facts the information in state registers of births, deaths and marriages, whereas these sources are full of errors.

Thirdly, one is given very little idea of the degree of success to be expected. How far back can one hope to trace a line? Glib references to the O'Neills of Ulster having the most ancient documented pedigree in Western Europe, and to other old Irish genealogies are misleading and no substitute for solid, well-researched fact. How much detail can one hope to get? When should one decide that one has reached the end of the line? None of these questions receives a satisfactory answer.

SOCIAL GROUP

A comprehensive guidebook covering all social groups would run into several volumes. This book aims to be both compact and relevant to as many people as possible, and so I have focused on the group from which the overwhelming majority of Irish people are descended.

Under pressure from English merchants and manufacturers the British parliament had so restricted Irish trade in the eighteenth century that the country was forced to rely upon agriculture. The landlords thus found themselves with a virtual monopoly of the means of livelihood. The French traveller Gustave de Beaumont wrote in 1839: 'The Catholic of Ireland finds only one profession within his reach, the culture of the soil.'

The 1841 census indicates that 66 per cent of all Irish families were 'chiefly employed in agriculture'. Under the broader heading: 'chiefly employed in agriculture plus proportion of other pursuits', the figure is raised to 73 per cent.

The 1861 census provided for the first time reliable figures of Church membership. Out of a population of five and three quarter million, four and a half million, or 77 per cent, were Catholics, under 700,000, or 12 per cent, were members of the Church of Ireland, and a little over half a million, or 9 per cent, were Presbyterians.

It is perfectly clear from these figures that Catholic tenant farmers and their families constituted the majority of the Irish population in the last century. It follows that most people with Irish blood in their veins, both at home and abroad, are descended from this group. I have concentrated therefore on tracing roots from the point of view of the man or woman descended from nineteenth-century Catholic tenant farmer stock. Of course, the Irish Catholic tenantry was, in itself, a very large and diverse group. At one extreme the proprietors of large grassland 'ranches' present a picture of prosperity and are almost indistinguishable from middlemen landlords. At the other extreme, the landless labourers who rented potato gardens from year to year from tenant farmers suffered grinding poverty.

The concentration on the Catholic tenantry does not mean

that there is nothing in this book for those descended from other social groups. The book is the most complete guide available to the twelve best sources of genealogical information. Only two of the record collections dealt with are exclusively agricultural; only one is exclusively Catholic.

2

SOURCES: GENERAL INFORMATION

Before dealing with genealogical sources, an understanding of the administrative divisions of Ireland is important. It is also useful to know a little of the history of Irish records.

ADMINISTRATIVE DIVISIONS

Of the ten administrative divisions most frequently referred to in this book, four are civil divisions of considerable antiquity: *County, Barony, Civil Parish* and *Townland*; four are associated with legislation introduced in the mid-nineteenth century: *Poor Law Union, Dispensary District, Superintendent Registrar's District* and *Registrar's District*; and two are ecclesiastical divisions: *Diocese* and *Parish*.

The *county* is the division with which people are most familiar. The creation by statute in 1606 of Wicklow finalized the county framework as we know it today. The county was and still is the principal unit of local government. Most collections of documents are organized on a county basis.

The *barony* is an important county subdivision. The usual number per county is seven to ten. Cork with twenty has the largest number; at the other end of the scale, Louth has only five. Occasionally a barony occupies part of two counties, in which case it is known as a half-barony in each. There are 331 baronies in Ireland. The origin of this particular division is unclear. It is thought to be Norman or pre-Norman. From the sixteenth to the nineteenth centuries it was utilized officially in surveys, land transactions, censuses, etc.

There are 2508 *civil parishes* in Ireland. They often break both barony and county boundaries. Originally, as the name implies, they were ecclesiastical divisions, but they became important civil divisions in time. They originated in the thirteenth century or in some cases even earlier.

The *townland* is the smallest administrative division in

8

Ireland and there are 60,462 of them in the country. The average townland size is about 350 acres, though individual size varies enormously – the smallest townland is a little over one acre while the largest is over 7000 acres. A difficulty which may crop up with townlands is that many have the same name. There are 56 Kilmores and 47 Dromores, for example. Knowing the name of the county and the barony in which the townland you are researching is situated usually overcomes this problem.

The Poor Law Act of 1838 introduced a new division to Ireland: the *poor law union*. The country was divided into 130 (later 163) poor law unions. Each of these districts was composed of multiples of townlands with a market town at the centre. A workhouse was built in the town for the relief of the destitute poor within the union. The property-holders within the union had to pay rates for the upkeep of the poor.

The Medical Charities Act of 1851 subdivided the poor law unions into *dispensary districts*. These same divisions were used in registering births and deaths. Each poor law union became, under the 1863 Acts for the Registration of Births, Deaths and Marriages, a *superintendent registrar's district*; each *dispensary district* became a registrar's district, of which there were 829.

The ecclesiastical divisions of the Church of Ireland are important when researching Catholic ancestry. The Church of Ireland was the Established or state Church and as such it carried out some duties normally associated with the civil power; notably, a religious survey in 1766 and the probating of all wills, both Catholic and Protestant, up to the year 1858, when a *principal registry* and eleven *district registries* were established for proving wills and granting administrations. The boundaries of Church of Ireland *dioceses* are much older than county divisions and they do not correspond with one another in any instance. There are 22 dioceses and four archdioceses. The dioceses are united to form the provinces of the four archbishops of Armagh, Dublin, Cashel and Tuam, and subdivided to form parishes.

While the Church of Ireland *parishes* are usually composed of amalgamations of the ancient civil parishes mentioned above, modern Catholic parishes show no such correspondence. The reason for this is that there was a break in continuity between

9

the medieval Church in Ireland and the modern Catholic Church. A period of severe persecution led to a breakdown in Catholic parochial organization. When the Church began to reorganize itself in the early nineteenth century, it based its new territorial divisions on the needs of the time rather than returning to its former pattern.

TWO STATES

Another aspect of Irish administrative divisions to be kept in mind is the complication that was created for researchers by the setting up of two Irish states: Northern Ireland in 1921 and the Irish Free State in 1922. As might be expected, records that had been accumulated over the previous centuries were, in some cases, divided between the two states. Some documents relating to the six northern counties – Down, Derry, Armagh, Antrim, Fermanagh and Tyrone – which had hitherto been held in Dublin, were despatched to the North. In the case of collections that were split, I have focused on the greater part of the collection, invariably held south of the border, and given the address of the northern repository where the remainder of the collection may be found. This procedure avoids repetition and is consistent with my aim of catering for the majority of those researching their roots.

CHANGING BOUNDARIES

A factor that the family historian may encounter is the problem of changing boundaries. The demarcation lines of the various administrative divisions may not have been stable over the entire time-span encompassed by his research.

Some townlands found in seventeenth-century surveys have disappeared due to amalgamation with other townlands, anglicization or changing of the original name. The Ordnance Survey created a number of new townlands, mostly by dividing existing ones. It is usually easy to identify these, as the new units retained the original name with the addition of adjectives like 'Upper', 'Lower', 'East', 'West', etc.

The fact that civil parishes originated as ecclesiastical parishes from which a rector derived an income would lead one to expect that these units remained largely unchanged, the tithes ensuring that land belonging to one parish would not be detached and given to another. However, in the course of his work on the Kenmare papers, Edward MacLysaght found that parish boundaries did change through the centuries.

Legislation in 1823 empowered grand juries to change boundaries of baronies. Some baronies were split into two or more parts; sections were sliced off and given to others.

Catholic parishes continued to develop and change during the nineteenth century. The creation of new parishes from parts of older parishes can be particularly confusing for the genealogist. This problem will be discussed later.

LOCATING ADMINISTRATIVE DIVISIONS

If you know the name of the townland and county from which the subject of your research came, it is easy, with the aid of a number of widely available reference books, to find the names of the other important administrative divisions, both civil and ecclesiastical, in which the townland is located.

The *General Alphabetical Index to the Townlands and Towns of Ireland*, published in 1901, lists alphabetically the names of all the townlands in Ireland and gives the following information about each one: the Ordnance Survey sheet number; the area in statute acres; the name of the county, barony and civil parish in which it is situated.

It also gives the *county district* and *district electoral division* of the townland. The Local Government Act of 1898 adopted the poor law union as the basic administrative division of Ireland in place of the civil parish and barony, but it changed the name of this administrative unit to 'county district'. Each county district was further divided into district electoral divisions, and townlands were arranged according to these divisions. Parishes and baronies were retained only as a means of making comparisons with statistics gathered prior to 1898. An earlier edition of the *Townland Index* published in 1877, prior to the Local Government Act, names the poor law union in which each townland is situated. The same information may be found in other pre-1898 editions of the *Townland Index*, notably, the *General Alphabetical Index to the Townlands and Towns, Parishes and Baronies of Ireland, Based on the Census of Ireland for the Year*

1851. This edition was reprinted in 1984 by the Genealogical Publishing Co., Inc., Baltimore, and is generally available in libraries.

The diocese, Church of Ireland parish and Catholic parish in which a townland is situated may be found by consulting *A Topographical Dictionary of Ireland*, by Samuel Lewis, which contains a short description of every civil parish in Ireland.

Irish Records: Sources for Family and Local History by James S. Ryan, Ph.D., is a valuable reference book of more recent publication. As well as helping to establish the Catholic parish in which each civil parish is situated, the book lists many of the available records for each county of Ireland. These are listed within each county and include the following: census and census substitutes, Roman Catholic Church records, gravestone inscriptions, wills and administrations, miscellaneous research sources and services. *A Guide to Irish Parish Registers*, by Brian Mitchell, is widely available. It gives information on the parish registers of all denominations.

A New Genealogical Atlas of Ireland, also by Brian Mitchell, was published in 1986 and is a very useful work. All 2508 civil parishes are mapped and clearly identifiable. Three maps for each county are included in the volume, by means of which six major administrative divisions are very easily located, namely: counties, baronies, civil parishes, dioceses, poor law unions and probate districts.

Occasionally it may be helpful to know the names of the townlands adjoining the area of your research, or to know their position in relation to the civil parish boundaries. This information can be ascertained by finding the townland on a map. In 1846 the Ordnance Survey completed a set of six inch to the mile maps for all Ireland. Full sets are available in the National Library and sets for individual counties are available in the respective county libraries.

DESTRUCTION OF RECORDS

Fire, carelessness and pilfering have been common causes of the loss and destruction of national archives in all countries, but Ireland has suffered more than its share in this respect.

Many of the records of the Court of Chancery were

consumed in 1304 when a fire broke out in St Mary's Abbey, their place of storage. In 1537 it was found that the keepers of records in Dublin Castle were so lax that they stole, or allowed others to steal, the records in their custody. Special arrangements were then made for the safekeeping of the records in the Bermingham Tower. This part of the Dublin Castle complex became almost the sole repository for government records, so when it was burned down in 1758 the loss was great indeed.

In 1711 a fire in the Custom House had destroyed many of the books belonging to the Surveyor General's office. The national archives were further depleted by the practice of the Lord Lieutenants, Chief Secretaries and various other top officials of treating government documents as their own private property and removing with them large quantities of papers when their time of office expired.

A great step forward was taken in 1810 with the appointment of a Commission of Public Records. During the twenty years of its existence it attempted a stock-taking of the national archives. This work entered a new phase with the passing of the Public Record (Ireland) Act in 1867, which allowed for the building of a Public Record Office.

Two structures were provided: one incorporating a public reading room and search room, and a separate record treasury. The treasury consisted of one huge apartment 140 feet long, 80 feet wide and 50 feet high. For the next 54 years the work of receiving and arranging national records went on.

On 1 April 1922 the British handed over the Public Record Office to the Provisional Government. Less than two weeks later it was occupied by Irregular Forces, who turned the record treasury into a bomb factory. Towards the end of June the Provisional Government decided to recapture the Four Courts complex, including the Public Record Office. With field guns borrowed from the British army they attacked the building. Under a headline remarkable for its spirit of non-partisanship: 'Regulars' Dashing Attack Irregulars' Fine Defence', the *Constitution* described the outcome:

Shortly after noon there occurred a terrific explosion at the Four Courts and this proved to be the beginning of the end. The explosion was of tremendous violence. Observers saw a great flame leap into the air. The atmosphere for some distance became dark, a thick pall of smoke hung over the dome which remains standing.The explosion took place in the rear of the building, large portions of which were destroyed. Debris was showered far around and charred documents of national records were picked up in the streets a mile away.

Indeed, it was reported later that some documents were found on the Hill of Howth, seven miles away. In a matter of seconds, two heavy mines, which had exploded in the record treasury, destroyed seven centuries of work.

Since this event, which can be described only as a great national tragedy, there have been efforts to make good the loss. Some of the gaps have been filled.

The Public Record Office is now known as the National Archives and it will be referred to by its new name throughout the rest of this book. This is not altogether satisfactory as the name National Archives is of fairly recent origin and many of my allusions to this institution date to times when it was known as the Public Record Office. However, it is hoped, by this procedure, to avoid greater confusion.

LOCATIONS OF RECORDS

At present, material in the National Archives is held at four different premises in Dublin: Bishop Street, the Four Courts, the State Paper Office in Dublin Castle, and Dominic Street Upper. In 1991 the headquarters of the National Archives will move from the Four Courts to Bishop Street. The reading room in the State Paper Office is to close, but the reading room in the Four Courts will remain open for the time being.

Important genealogical sources are held at other locations also. The following is a list of addresses of the archives mentioned in chapter 3:

National Archives,
58-64 Dominic Street Upr,
Dublin 7

National Archives,
Four Courts,
Dublin 7

Registry of Deeds,
Henrietta Street,
Dublin 1

Valuation Office,
6 Ely Place,
Dublin 2

General Register Office of
  Northern Ireland,
Oxford House,
49-55 Chichester Street,
Belfast BT1 4H6

Land Commission,
24 Merrion Street,
Dublin 2

Public Record Office of
  Northern Ireland,
66 Balmoral Avenue,
Belfast BT9 6NY

General Register Office of
  Ireland,
Joyce House,
8-11 Lombard Street East,
Dublin 2

National Library of Ireland,
Kildare Street,
Dublin 2

Genealogical Office.
2 Kildare Street,
Dublin 2

3

TWELVE MAJOR SOURCES

The Pareto Principle, named after an Italian social scientist, states that significant items in a given group normally constitute a relatively small portion of the entire group. The concept is often referred to as the 80/20 rule. It has a wide application. Thus in a discussion group 20 per cent of the people will do 80 per cent of the talking; in a classroom 20 per cent of the pupils will take up 80 per cent of the teacher's time. The Pareto Principle applies to family history in this way: 80 per cent of the records refer to a mere 20 per cent of the people. The corollary: that only 20 per cent of all documentary material is relevant as far as 80 per cent of the people are concerned, unfortunately seems to be broadly true.

Government surveys like the Strafford Survey, the Civil Survey, the Down Survey, the 'census' of 1659, the Books of Survey and Distribution, concern landowners of the seventeenth century and not the common people who worked the land. Newspapers, periodicals, directories and almanacs are relevant, for the most part, to those in trades and professions, industry and commerce. Court records and state papers, military, naval and police records undoubtedly impinge upon the members of the group under discussion, occasionally. However, to go into detail about police records, for example, in order to facilitate research on tenant farmers' sons who joined the RIC, would be to burden most readers with useless information.

In the following pages I have attempted to describe every major documentary source which offers a reasonable possibility of yielding ancestral information concerning the Irish Catholic tenant farmer: that is, the group from which perhaps 75 per cent of Irish people are descended. Of the twelve sources examined, six are very likely to be productive, namely: census returns, civil registration, parish records, land commission records, *Griffith's Valuation* and the tithe applotment books. The other six: estate records, wills, the Registry of Deeds, the Religious Census of 1766, hearth money rolls and gravestone inscriptions, are less sure, either because those being researched may not have been included in the records, or because the relevant parts of the records were destroyed.

It is useful to know the original purpose of the records you are examining. It is essential to know where the documents are to be found, how they are indexed, what information you need to know before you can locate a relevant entry and to what extent particular records are likely to further your researches. With this in mind, I will describe, in their historical context, the twelve categories of documents mentioned.

I

CENSUS RETURNS AND RELATED MATERIAL

The best-known census is that carried out under the Emperor Augustus: 'It happened that a decree went out at this time from the Emperor Augustus, enjoining that the whole world should be registered . . . and Joseph, being of David's clan and family, came up from the town of Nazareth, in Galilee, to . . . the city called Bethlehem, to give his name there.' (Luke 2: 1-5.)

Population counts were reported in ancient Japan and were made by Egyptians, Greeks, Hebrews, Persians, and in Peru, long before the arrival of Europeans. The oldest continuous periodic census is that of the United States. The decennial census was started there in 1790, in compliance with Article l, section 2 of the Constitution, which provides that the representation in Congress shall be in proportion to the population and that this shall be adjusted in accordance with the census to be taken every ten years.

However, if we were to define the modern census as one in which information is gathered about each individual rather than each household, then the modern census began in Ireland in 1821.

On 28 May of that year, enumerators started to call on every household in Ireland, extending their work into subsequent days if necessary. They were to ascertain the name, age, occupation and relationship to the head of the household of every member of each household. They were also to record the acreage held by each householder and the number of storeys in each dwelling-house. The statistical society of London held this census to have been by far the most perfect in its machinery and methods of any that had yet been executed in these islands. The subsequent decennial censuses were all successful. Those from 1841 to 1871 were in some respects unrivalled by those of any other country.

An earlier census had been attempted in Ireland in 1813, but the results were neither printed nor presented to parliament. The failure was due to a number of factors: some counties refused to participate; enumerators qualified by being Protestant – illiteracy did not debar them – and were paid according to the number they returned, so there was a tendency to exaggerate; the peasantry was suspicious and refused to co-operate, as it was held that the census would facilitate the press gang, taxation and the general oppression of the people. The whole scheme was abandoned in 1815.

Despite the Act of Union, the British and Irish census procedures were quite different. The first British census was taken in 1801 and the process was repeated every ten years. The first four British censuses recorded only numbers, and though the 1841 census did record names, it is very short on further information. The British returns for 1801, 1811, 1821 and 1831 were destroyed as they contained only statistical material. All the others were preserved in the Public Record Office, Chancery Lane, London. In contrast with the British procedure, the Irish census returns for 1861, 1871, 1881 and 1891 were destroyed by government order. The Irish census returns for the years 1813, 1821, 1831, 1841 and 1851 were preserved in the National Archives, Dublin, where they were destroyed in the explosion and fire of 1922. This great collection, which named and gave details of every man, woman and child alive in Ireland through most of the first half of the nineteenth century, was the saddest loss in that holocaust of Irish history.

Some few fragments of these returns were saved. Rosemary ffolliot lists them by county in *Irish Genealogy: A Record Finder*. They may also be found in James G. Ryan's *Irish Records: Sources for Family and Local History*.

After the introduction of old age pensions in 1908, the census returns for 1841 and 1851 were used by many people to establish the fact that they were over 70 years of age and thus entitled to a pension. Since registration of births did not begin until 1864, birth certificates were not available for this purpose. Proof of age could be obtained in a variety of ways – through searches in parish registers or army records, for example, but for many, census returns were the only possible means. Applicants who wished to get proof of age in this way sent details to the National Archives where a search was carried out. When the family was found and the applicant identified as a child of the family, a certified copy of the return was issued giving the name, age, parentage and birth-place of the person concerned – on payment of two shillings. Census search forms or 'green forms' – some of which, paradoxically, are pink – were completed by the staff of the National Archives between 1910 and 1922. In 1911 alone, over 85,000 such searches were carried out. The forms were kept by local agencies of the Customs and Excise Department. In 1928 the forms relating to the Twenty-Six Counties were returned to the National Archives in Dublin, where they originated. Those relating to the Six Counties were sent to the Public Record Office of Northern Ireland.

There is a 'green form' index for each county in the National Archives. Each index is arranged by barony, civil parish and townland. When a townland appears in the index, the name of each individual resident is given on whose behalf a 'green form' was filled. Little effort is involved in locating 'green forms'.

The 1901 and 1911 census returns were stored locally in 1922 and were thus saved from destruction. They have been transferred to the National Archives and are available for examination. Census returns after 1911 are not available. From the point of view of family history, the 1901 and 1911 censuses deal with a comparatively recent period, but they may be worth examining to establish quickly some hard facts like marital status, number and names of children, address, etc. It should be noted, however, that ages of adults are highly unreliable in census returns. The expectation that people will be recorded as having aged ten years between the 1901 and the 1911 censuses is often not fulfilled.

The 1901 census forms have been bound in townland volumes, each numbered. The 1901 version of the *Townland Index* lists these numbers after the townlands in the column headed 'No. in Table vii of Census County Book, 1901'. This number and the name of the county is sufficient for the archivist to procure the appropriate volume. Some libraries have microfilms of census returns for their own region, so it may not be necessary to go to the National Archives to carry out this kind of research.

The published reports of the various Irish censuses can be of great assistance to the family historian. Of particular importance is the publication from 1841 to 1911 of the area, population, number of houses and valuation of each individual townland in Ireland. Knowing the exact number of people and the exact number of houses in a townland is a help in evaluating much of the information that a family historian is likely to gather. Probably the most useful of the series is *The Census of Ireland for the Year 1851, showing the area, population and number of houses by Townland and Electoral Divisions.* This shows the townland figures for both 1841 and 1851 – immediately before and immediately after the famine. It is readily available in libraries as it was reprinted in facsimile form in 1968 by the Irish University Press, titled *British Parliamentary Papers, 1851, Census Ireland Population, 12.*

II

STATE REGISTRATION
OF BIRTHS, DEATHS AND MARRIAGES

Everyone is familiar with the birth certificate, a document detailing the basic facts about one's birth, authenticated by the signature and stamp of the superintendent registrar and bearing the stern warning that 'to alter this document or to utter it so altered is a serious offence'. For our present purposes it is necessary to subject that common document to a detailed scrutiny. If you have the longer form of your birth certificate to hand (alternatively, see Figure 1), you will see that it states your date of birth, your first name and sex, your mother's maiden name, your father's name, address and occupation. It also gives the signature, qualification and residence of the person who informed the registrar of your birth and the signature of the official who registered it. Closer examination will show that the certificate also reveals the source of all this information. The superintendent registrar's signature is appended to this statement: 'I hereby certify that the foregoing is a true Copy of the entry No. . . . in a Register Book of Births'. At the head of the certificate is to be found the name of the county and the name of the division of the superintendent registrar's district in which the birth was originally registered. To get a copy of your own birth certificate you must present the registrar with sufficient information to enable him to locate the appropriate entry in the appropriate register book. He will then simply transcribe the information onto the standard form, sign it and stamp it for an appropriate fee. Companion documents, the death and marriage certificates, have a similar genesis.

State registration of all births, deaths and marriages began in Ireland on New Year's Day 1864. (Registration of non-Catholic marriages began in 1845.) I have already detailed the information recorded in birth registers. Death registers noted the following information: date and place of death, name and

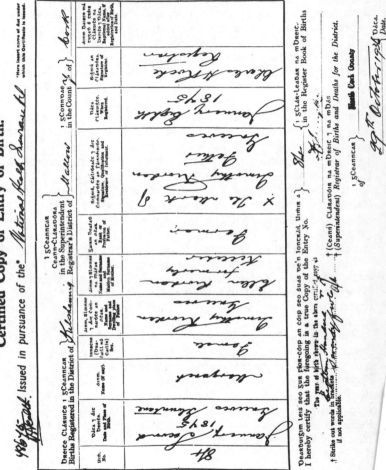

Figure 1: Birth certificate of Margaret Riordan

surname, sex , marital status, age, rank, profession or occupation, cause of death and duration of illness, date of registration, signature, address and qualification of informant. Marriage register books recorded the date of the marriage, the names of the couple, their ages, marital status, their rank or professions, their residence at the time of marriage, the names and occupations of their fathers. These register books are of great interest to the family historian, considering the wealth of detail in them. The year 1864 may appear to be a rather late date of commencement. However, deaths recorded in the 1860s and 1870s are often of people born in the previous century. The names and occupations of the bride and groom's fathers are also valuable pieces of information that may not be available so easily elsewhere. We must now turn our attention to the problem of locating in those registers the entries concerning those of our ancestors whom we are researching.

Under the Poor Law Act of 1838 and its various amendments Ireland had been divided into 163 poor law unions. Each union had a large town like Macroom or Mallow at its centre in which a workhouse was built. Owners and occupiers of property within a union were required to pay rates for the upkeep of the poor within that union. The Medical Charities Act of 1851 divided each union into dispensary districts. The poor law union of Macroom, for example, had five dispensary districts: Slievereagh, Macroom, Inchigeela, Connaway and Clonmoyle.

The Act for the Registration of Births and Deaths proposed to make use of these recently created administrative divisions. The Act states: 'Every Union that shall have been formed by the Poor Law Commissioners, under the provisions of the Acts for the Relief of the Destitute Poor Ireland, shall, from and after the said Thirty-first day of December 1863, be a Superintendent Registrar's District . . . Each Dispensary District of a Poor Law Union shall, with the approval of the Registrar-General, be a Registrar's District.'

The Act goes on to prescribe a three-tier system of registration. A registrar – operating on the lowest tier – registered births and deaths within his registrar's district: that is, the original dispensary district. Every quarter he sent certified

copies of his registers to his immediate superior, the superintendent registrar, who was in charge of registration within the entire union. Each time a registrar filled a book, he also sent that to his superintendent registrar.

The superintendent registrar of a union sent certified copies of the registers in his possession to the Registrar-General – the official in Dublin in overall charge of registration. He retained the original registers himself. He was obliged to make indexes of the register books in his possession and to allow persons to search them on payment of a fee.

The Registrar-General was to: 'cause indexes of all Registers herein mentioned to be made and kept in the General Register Office; and every Person shall be entitled to search the said Indexes between the Hours of Ten in the Morning and Four in the Afternoon'.

It is clear from the above that the original records were to be held locally by the 163 superintendent registrars throughout the country; that the Registrar-General was to hold copies of all registers; and that both sets of records were to be made available to the public. Apart from a tendency towards greater centralization, the system has changed little since its commencement in 1864. In the county of Cork, for example, the original registers are now held in three locations – Cork, Mallow and Skibbereen, instead of the original 20 poor law unions. The Kerry registers are held in Killarney instead of the original five poor law unions.

The provincial births, deaths and marriages registration offices are now under the jurisdiction of the various health boards throughout the country. Their addresses may be found easily in the green pages at the start of all telephone directories, under the appropriate health boards. The records of the Registrar-General are kept at Joyce House, 8/11 Lombard Street East, Dublin.

From the researcher's point of view there are some important differences between the locally held records and those held centrally. Superintendent registrars indexed each individual register, whereas the Registrar-General had responsibility for preparing alphabetical indexes of births, deaths and marriages on a countrywide basis for each year. A researcher who goes to the central office in Joyce House is permitted to examine the indexes to the records only and not the records themselves. Researchers who go along to the provincial offices are normally allowed to examine the original register books. Some provincial offices are too small to permit members of the public to carry out research there. In these cases, the staff of the offices undertake to do the research for a fee.

Whether to do research at local level or centrally depends on the information you have. If you are unable to establish the name of the registrar's district in which a birth, death or marriage took place, then the name and year indexes in Joyce House are your only option. However, once you know the name of the district, the local office will be found to be more productive.

In the registers of births, deaths and marriages, the townland is the only address given for people from the countryside. If you know the name of the townland in which a birth, death or marriage took place, you can easily find out which superintendent registrar's district it is in by consulting the 1877 edition of the *Alphabetical Index to the Townlands and Towns of Ireland*. This book will indicate which poor law union the townland is in. The superintendent registrar's district and the poor law union are identical divisions.

Once you have enough information both to locate the entries you are looking for and to identify them when you find them, you are ready to write, phone or personally call to the appropriate provincial office. On payment of a fee, the staff will allow you to spend the day researching the register books of whatever registrar's district you are interested in. There were about 830 of these districts in the country, so, as units of population, they are not too big to handle.

It is not difficult to piece together the salient facts concerning a family by consulting these registers. The discovery of one birth can lead to those of brothers and sisters and to the marriage entry of the parents. An added bonus for the researcher is the section headed 'signature, qualification and residence of informant'. These days the informant tends to be a member of the medical profession or a hospital official, as births and deaths normally take place in hospitals with doctors in attendance. This was not the case for much of the period of state registration; a member of the family normally acted as the informant. Many of the informants were illiterate and put their mark 'X' between their first name and surname, which was written by the registrar on their behalf. If the informant could write, it is interesting to look at the signature of a long-dead ancestor. Such a signature is, perhaps, the only identifiable piece of work to have survived many a man or woman from the past.

If you do not wish to do the research personally, the staff of the superintendent registrar will do it for a fee. The cost of certificates is very high, and certified copies are not normally required for the purposes of family history. It is therefore more economical to write with a request for information rather than for certificates.

The situation in the North of Ireland is significantly different. The original register books of births and deaths going back as far as 1864 and the original marriage register books from 1922 are all held at the central office in Belfast. Pre-1922 marriage records are held at local government offices throughout the Six Counties. Indexes of births from 1864 and indexes of deaths and marriages from 1922 are also available at the Belfast office. Members of the public are allowed to examine the indexes but are not allowed to touch the original books. Searches may be carried out in the original registers by telephoning to make an appointment and confirming this appointment in writing. On payment of a small fee you are allocated a member of staff for a period of six hours. The staff member will handle the books and help you with your research. The office has come under a great deal of pressure as interest in family history has increased, so you are likely to have a six-month wait for an appointment.

A certificate of birth, death or marriage is an imposing-looking document. Its official appearance is inclined to persuade one to accept that its contents are true. Unfortunately, this is often not the case. In fact, as already stated, these certificates do not even claim to carry correct information. A certificate purports to be a true copy of an entry in a register book. The copy cannot be more accurate than the original entry, the veracity of which depends on the informant.

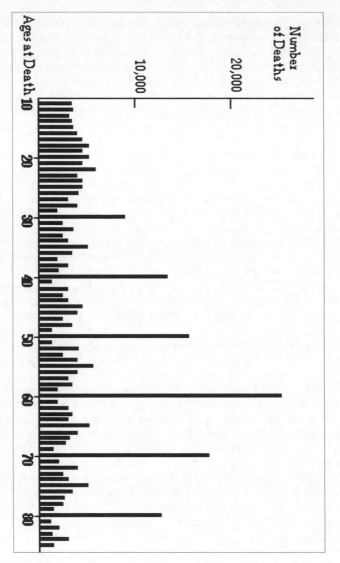

Figure 2: Chart showing ages at death, based
on 1841 census returns

The most common inaccuracies are the ages given in death certificates. I have found some of these to be mistaken by up to ten years. No reliance should be placed on ages in death certificates unless the informant is a person who might be expected to know the exact age of the deceased. A powerful demonstration of how inaccurate people tended to be in recording age at death can be found in the graph reproduced as Figure 2. It is based on information given in 1841 census returns. Heads of families were asked to write in the ages at death of family members who had died since the previous census. It appears from the spikes on the graph that adults tended to die in large numbers when they attained ages ending with a zero. The ages of 40 and 50 seemed to be particularly dangerous. Of course, the real explanation of this phenomenon is that heads of families rounded ages of dead family members to the nearest decimal. Only the ages of dead children appear to have been faithfully recorded. Ages in marriage certificates, when given, are often inaccurate also.

I found significant mistakes in three out of five birth register entries that I examined in relation to one particular family. In one entry, the mother's maiden name was incorrect. The informant, the grandmother of the baby, gave her own maiden name. The address was incorrect in a second entry. In the third, a male child, with an obviously male name, was entered in the register as a female. Fourteen years later the entry was corrected, probably when the individual concerned went to get a birth certificate in connection with a job. Errors could be clerical, or the result of faulty information being given by informants.

More serious than errors are omissions. It is impossible to estimate the number of births and deaths that went unregistered. Even though there was a fine of twenty shillings for failure to give notice of a birth or death, there is evidence that births, especially in the early years, often went unregistered. Frequent examples of applicants for old age pensions in the 1930s and 1940s who found it difficult to establish their claims verify this point.

It is equally difficult to quantify the number of marriages that were never registered. In 1861 the Registrar-General of England thought that the clergy of the Church of England were careless in recording marriages. It is hard to say whether the Irish Catholic clergy were similarly careless in this area.

Before leaving civil registration, it is worth mentioning the *Special Report on Surnames in Ireland*, prepared by Robert E. Matheson and issued in 1894 as an appendix to the annual report of the Registrar-General. The report lists every surname for which five or more births were recorded in the year 1890. The names are listed alphabetically in tabular form. The facsimile reproduced as Figure 3 is typical of the whole.

The birth rate in Ireland in 1890 was one in 44.8. A fairly accurate estimate of the number of people bearing a particular surname may be made by multiplying the figures given by Matheson for that name by 44.8. For the less frequently occurring surnames, the accuracy of this procedure cannot be depended upon.

The great value of the *Special Report* is that it indicates how common a surname is countrywide, provincially, and within a county. Writing in 1950, Edward MacLysaght stated that the distribution of surnames had not altered materially since the publication of the *Special Report*. To assume that the same pattern existed for a considerable time before 1890 – a period with which we are more concerned – does not seem unreasonable. Knowing how common a surname is in a particular area facilitates the family historian in making certain decisions and assumptions. If a particular surname is very common, it might be considered more productive to divert attention to another branch of the family tree. In the case of a rare surname, the criteria for verifying whether the name found is the person sought may be less rigorous.

The *Special Report* is relatively easy to obtain. Apart from its initial publication as an appendix to the twenty-ninth annual report of the Registrar-General, it was also issued in the same year as a separate booklet, priced at seven and a half pence. There was a reissue in 1909. It may be found in any of these forms in city and county libraries. It has appeared again recently as chapter 10 of *Irish Genealogy: A Record Finder*, with an introduction by Donal F. Begley.

Table showing the Surnames in Ireland having Five Entries and Upwards in the Birth Indexes of 1890, together with the Number in each Registration Province, and the Registration Counties in which these Names are principally found—*continued.*

Names.	NUMBER OF ENTRIES IN BIRTH INDEXES FOR 1890.					Counties in which principally found.
	IRELAND.	Leinster.	Munster.	Ulster.	Connaught	
*Mulkerrin (5),	10	-	-	1	9	9 in Galway.
*Mullally (8),	14	7	5	1	1	—
*Mullan (92)—Mullen (72)—Mullin (53).	218	39	2	128	49	Tyrone, Londonderry, Galway and Antrim.
Mullane,	31	-	29	-	2	16 in Cork and 8 in Limerick.
*Mullany (27),	32	1	7	2	22	Roscommon, Mayo, and Sligo.
Mullarkey,	21	-	-	1	20	Mayo, Galway, and Sligo.
Mulligan,	105	32	1	34	38	Dublin, Mayo, and Monaghan.
Mullins,	47	8	35	-	4	Cork and Clare.
Mulqueen,	6	-	6	-	-	4 in Limerick and 2 in Clare.
Mulrennan,	5	1	-	-	4	—
Mulroe,	5	-	-	-	5	3 in Mayo and 2 in Galway.
*Mulrooney (9),	12	4	1	-	7	—
Mulroy,	12	2	-	-	10	10 in Mayo.
Mulry,	5	-	-	1	4	Galway.
*Mulvany (4)—Mulvanny (4).	15	12	-	2	1	—
Mulvenna,	5	-	-	5	-	All in Antrim.
*Mulvey (21),	27	3	4	1	19	13 in Leitrim.
*Mulvihill (15),	21	4	12	1	4	Kerry and Limerick.
Murdock (18)—Murdoch (12).	30	2	1	27	-	Antrim.
*Murnane (13)	14	4	10	-	-	Limerick and Cork.
*Murphy (1385),	1386	476	611	189	110	Generally distributed, but the largest numbers are found in Cork, Dublin, and Wexford. They vary from 5 in each of the counties of Westmeath, Tyrone, and Sligo, to close on 500 in Cork.
*Murray (405),	438	120	65	161	92	Dublin, Antrim, Cork, Down, Galway, and Mayo. There is no County, however, without representatives of this name.
*Murrin (6),	8	5	-	1	2	—
*Murtagh (58),	66	30	1	17	18	Dublin and Sligo.
*Myers (10),	11	4	4	3	-	Wexford and Antrim.
Myles (7)—Miles (5),	12	7	3	2	-	
*Nagle (32),	39	3	32	3	1	Cork.
Nally,	20	4	-	-	16	Mayo and Roscommon.
Napier,	8	-	-	8	-	Antrim and Down.
*Nash (20),	21	5	15	-	1	Kerry and Limerick.
*Naughton (52),	71	1	19	1	50	Galway, Mayo, Roscommon, and Clare.
Navin,	6	1	-	-	5	Mayo.
*Naylor (5),	6	4	-	2	-	Dublin.
Neal (6)—Neale (4),	10	7	1	2	-	—
*Neary (34),	43	12	2	2	27	Mayo, Roscommon, Dublin, and Louth.
Nee,	17	1	1	-	15	15 in Galway.
Needham,	7	-	1	1	5	5 in Mayo.
*Neely (9),	12	-	-	11	1	—
Neenan,	7	1	6	-	-	Clare.
Neeson,	17	-	-	17	-	Antrim.
*Neilan (12)—Nilan (7),	36	3	9	-	24	Galway, Roscommon, and Sligo.
*Neill (215)	244	97	78	63	6	Antrim, Cork, Kerry, Carlow, Dublin, and Wexford.
Nelis,	5	-	-	3	2	Londonderry and Mayo.
Nelson,	72	8	2	59	3	Antrim, Down, Londonderry, and Tyrone.
*Nesbitt (25),	30	5	1	23	1	Antrim, Armagh, and Dublin.
*Nestor (13),	15	2	5	-	8	Galway and Clare.
*Neville (36),	39	8	27	4	-	Limerick and Cork.
*Nevin (23),	23	8	2	5	8	—
*Newell (31),	34	2	1	27	4	Down and Antrim.
Newman,	36	13	20	3	-	Cork, Meath, and Dublin—15 in Cork.
*Neylon (10),	13	1	11	-	-	11 in Clare.

Figure 3: Facsimile of page 63 of Matheson's
Special Report on Surnames in Ireland

31

III

CATHOLIC PARISH RECORDS

Baptisms and marriages are the events recorded in Catholic parish registers. Baptism entries record the date of baptism, the baby's name, the name of his/her father, the mother's maiden name and the names of the two sponsors. Sometimes, but by no means always, the address of the family was given in the form of the townland in which they lived. Marriage entries record the date of marriage, the names of the bride and groom and the names of their witnesses. Again, the names of the townlands from which the contracting parties came may or may not be given.

Marriages normally took place in the bride's home and were recorded in the parish of the bride. Baptisms took place in the church. Because there was a time lapse between the solemnizing of a marriage and the entry of the details in the parish register, marriage entries are more prone to error than baptismal entries.

Beyond what is said above, it is not wise to generalize too much about Catholic parish registers. They vary, not only in the amount of information they give, but also in their date of commencement and their legibility. There was no legislation at all relating to Catholic parish registers. The Penal Laws made the keeping of registers a very difficult matter, as many parishes had no permanent churches. In rural Ireland few parish registers began before the end of the eighteenth century; in poorer parts of the country, notably, some west of Ireland counties, records did not commence until the mid-nineteenth century.

Three factors combine to make the registers difficult to read. Their physical condition is often quite poor, due to dampness and paper of inferior quality; the handwriting in some registers is often illegible, and some are written in Latin. Though the same formula is repeated in each entry and easily translated, an added difficulty is the tendency to render into Latin both

Christian names and surnames. The use of case-inflections in this process makes immediate identification of names quite difficult. The baptism of William McCarthy, Liscullane, son of Charles McCarthy and Ellen Dineen, was recorded in the following manner: 'Mensis Maii 1987, 25 die: Ego A. O'Sullivan Baptizavit Gulielmum filium legitimum Caroli McCarthy et Ellena Dineen ab Liscullane.'

The National Library of Ireland has microfilmed most Catholic parish registers and they are available for inspection at the National Library. Some registers in the Dublin area have not been filmed. The written consent of the parish priest must be obtained before examining the microfilms of the parishes within the following dioceses: Ardagh and Clonmacnoise, Cloyne, Down and Connor, Galway, Kerry and Limerick. The name and address of the parish priest may be found in *The Catholic Directory*, which is published annually and located in most city and county libraries.

An index of parish register microfilms is to hand at the desk in the reading room of the National Library. Under each diocese the parishes are listed alphabetically, together with the missing years or gaps, up to 1880, when microfilmed records end. Similar information may be found in Ryan's *Irish Records: Sources for Family and Local History* and the Heraldic Artists' *Handbook on Irish Genealogy*.

Experience has shown that these lists should not be regarded as infallible but should be taken as a guide. When I was researching a family that lived in the parish of Ballyvourney, I was informed locally that the records from 1810 to 1871 had been damaged by flood and that a great amount of material from that period was lost. The microfilm in the National Library of the Ballyvourney parish records lists the baptisms from 11 April 1825 to 29 December 1829 and goes on to state that 'other registers of this parish were destroyed by fire'. Some time later I found the baptisms of the parish of Ballyvourney from 1810 to 1868, fully listed in volume eleven of a series of books entitled *O'Kief Coshe Mang*, after the following statement:

Between 15 and 20 years ago the editor made a trip to Ballyvourney to trace family records, his grandmother Johanna Lucey having been born there. Fragments of an old book were found in the Rectory in which pages were scattered on several shelves and in a state of considerable disorder. In order to trace his own family . . . the various sheets were put together and were all copied . . . It is not known whether these scattered pages have ever been bound or microfilmed and the following records are presented with the hope that they will fill in some gaps in the local history of North and West Cork.

A more common cause of error is failing to take cognizance of the fact that some parishes were formed out of portions of older ones. Both the *Handbook of Irish Genealogy* and *Irish Records: Sources for Family and Local History* give the year 1866 as the date of commencement of the parish records of Spa, Co. Kerry. Since state registration of births, deaths and marriages commenced in 1864, it would appear that the area covered by the parish of Spa has no useful parish records. However, when I checked with the parish priest of Spa, I found out that the parish had been formed in 1866 out of portions of Ardfert parish, where records commenced in 1819, and Tralee parish, where records – in common with many urban areas – began in the eighteenth century, in the year 1772. When the records of a parish are listed as beginning at an unusually late period, it is worth checking to see if the date given is merely technically correct, being the year the parish was formed.

Over the last few years, the work of typing and indexing Catholic parish registers has been going on with the assistance of public money. The registers in this far more convenient form are held at local heritage centres and are not available to the public. It is envisaged that each county will eventually have a heritage centre with a staff employed to handle family history questions from the public.

IV

LAND COMMISSION RECORDS

The Land Commission began its work on the day the Land League was made illegal. It was, and still is, based in Mornington House, 24 Merrion Street, Dublin – one of the houses which claims to be the birthplace of the Duke of Wellington. Its primary purpose was to fix fair rents where disputes existed between landlords and tenants. In its archive, estimated at 6,000,000 documents, there are 530,000 fair rent orders and agreements. These are arranged by county and filed in boxes and volumes.

In addition to working as a court of arbitration, the Land Commission had entrusted to it the further duty of making loans from public funds to tenants who wished to become the owners of their farms. In time, this became its chief function. The bulk of its archive is related to land purchase.

Before ownership of the land was transferred from the landlord to the tenants, under the various Land Purchase Acts 1881 to 1923, the estate was examined by Land Commission surveyors. They listed the tenants and their acreages and prepared maps showing the boundaries of each farm. These surveys are known as 'Schedules of Areas'.

'Inspectors' Reports and Schedules' were drawn up for each estate. These documents certified that the land being transferred was good value for money and therefore suitable security for the loans being given to the tenants by the Land Commission. They also indicated the amount of rent being paid by each tenant and the annuity the tenant would have to pay the Land Commission after purchasing his farm.

Documents of title form a significant part of the collection. They consist of a description of the lands being sold and an abstract of the vendor's title to this land. Deeds, wills, mortgages and the like are also included to prove the statements made in the abstract. Though the most ancient documents, some of seventeenth-century origin, are to be found in this category, they tend to be of no relevance to the tenantry. Documents of purchase consist of the agreements signed by both the vendor and purchaser. These are the legal instruments which transferred the ownership of the land from the landlord to the tenant, while recognizing the Land Commission's interest.

Mr Edward Keane carried out a special survey of the Land Commission records for the National Library in the 1970s. He examined 8447 boxes of documents containing papers relating to 9343 estates. He then wrote a brief report on each estate. Typically, a report focuses on the documents of title and makes no reference to the standard documents which occur with each estate, such as the tenants' purchase agreements.

Mr Keane's reports are bound in numbered volumes and are available for examination at the National Library. The volumes are keyed to two card indexes. The 'Topographical Index' is made up of a collection of cards, one for each estate. They are arranged in the alphabetical order of the vendor's name, within baronies, within counties. The 'Names Index' consists of cards arranged in a single alphabet of names of vendors. Each card names the baronies in which the estate of the vendor in question lay and gives the estate number. Using this number, the summary description of estate documents may be found in the bound volumes.

If you wish to examine the documents mentioned in the summary description, it is necessary to write to the Keeper of Records, Land Commission, Agriculture House, Kildare Street, Dublin, naming the estate you are interested in and requesting an appointment to look at the material.

The Land Commission still functions as a section of the Department of Agriculture and it is not really geared to facilitate researchers. Its staff has been halved in recent years and the number of research queries that can be dealt with has, of necessity, been restricted. There are 16,000 boxes of documents stored at the offices of the Land Commission. Much of the material is jumbled and uncalendared. I have found research in this area helpful only insofar as it yields very good detail about farms. However, the information tends to deal with a past so recent as to render it of little use.

V

VALUATION AND POOR LAW RECORDS

When the 'Act for the More Effectual Relief of the Destitute Poor in Ireland' – commonly known as the 'Poor Law Act' – was passed in 1838, it became the first statutory social service to be implemented throughout the whole country. It was introduced to deal with the poorest and most destitute people in Ireland. From its original narrow social base it expanded to become the major source of Ireland's social services.

The workings of the Poor Law generated a great quantity of documentary material of interest to the genealogist. Before examining this body of work, it might be useful to review the Poor Law and the context in which it was enacted.

In the opening decades of the nineteenth century, approximately one-third of the people of Ireland were as destitute as those in Third World countries today. The Royal Commission of Enquiry into the Conditions of the Poorer Classes in Ireland, set up in 1833, reported that 2,385,000 people were in need of relief from poverty. The Commission found the living conditions of the labouring classes to be primitive in the extreme. The cottages had as flooring the bare earth on which they were built. No measures were taken against rising damp. The floors were often wet, due to holes in the thatch. About half the cottages were without chimneys of any kind. The smoke circulated through the building before being discharged through a hole in the thatch or through the front door. Seventy per cent of labourers' cottages were without beds. When a bed was available, the parents often shared it with four or five children, who could be up to eighteen years of age. Bed or no bed, at night the family had to huddle together for warmth. Some families had a whole blanket, but the majority had only a half-blanket, so they used their day clothes spread over them for warmth. Food commonly consisted of dry potatoes. These were often so scarce that the poor had to limit themselves to one meal per day. Mendicancy was the only course open to the destitute in Ireland: medevialism with few of the compensations of faith.

The poor in England and Wales were far better cared for than their Irish counterparts. An Elizabethan poor law made their upkeep chargeable to the parish to which they belonged. In 1795 the magistrates of Speenhamland in Berkshire introduced a system of outdoor relief to counter distress among agricultural labourers. They supplemented wages with rate aid to a minimum scale related to the price of bread and the size of the family. The Speenhamland system spread rapidly, especially in the south of England. Predictably it tended to depress wages and increase poor rates. There was widespread belief in the 1830s that many able-bodied men and women found it more attractive to live off the parish than to find employment. The 'Poor Law Amendment Act (1834)' was designed to force the poor to find work by terminating outdoor relief and replacing it with a workhouse system. Under this legislation a poor person could get relief only if he entered the workhouse with his entire family. This was known as the 'all or nothing principle'. To ensure that the poor would not flock to the workhouses, life in these institutions was quite deliberately made very unattractive. Conditions were to be worse than those of the lowest-paid worker outside. The Act, therefore, was founded on the premise that there was employment for those who were willing to work.

The situation with regard to the poor in Ireland was quite different. Outdoor relief was not being abused as it did not exist; nor was there any prospect of forcing the poor into employment because there were no jobs. Despite this, despite the advice of a government committee set up to examine the problem of poverty in Ireland, which rejected the workhouse system as a solution, and despite objections from many quarters, the British government decided to extend the workhouse system to Ireland.

The Poor Law Act of 1838 divided Ireland into unions. Each union was to have a workhouse. There were 130 unions at first, but later this number was increased to 163. In each union, a board of guardians was to be elected by the ratepayers to administer the Poor Law. It was to levy a compulsory rate in the union to finance the administration of poor relief. The granting of aid was to be at the discretion of the guardians so no destitute person had a statutory right to relief. A central authority, the Poor Law Commissioners for England and Wales, was to have overall control in implementing the provisions of the Act.

It was part of the philosophy of the workhouse system that life should be unpleasant for the inmates. This was achieved by a very strict, sometimes almost inhuman, regime. Families were immediately broken upon entry to the workhouse. There were separate, self-contained quarters for men, women, boys and girls. Relatives could be reunited for a while on Sundays. The duties of the master of the workhouse included allowing 'none who are capable of employment to be idle at any time'.

The daily routine involved rising for breakfast at 6 a.m., continuous monotonous work, meals eaten in silence and going to bed in a cold, overcrowded, unsanitary dormitory with lights out at 9 p.m.

A few residential institutions, supported by local taxation, for the upkeep of the destitute poor pre-dated the Poor Law. Those in Cork and Dublin were absorbed by the new system. The conversion of the House of Industry in Cork gave the Cork Union the distinction of being the first workhouse in Ireland to open its doors. It became operational from 15 February 1840, some six weeks before the North and South Dublin Unions. The inmates found the new regime too tough and there was a mass exodus from the institution. The workhouses, then, were places of last resort, an option to be considered only by the utterly destitute as an alternative to starvation.

A workhouse inmate was officially known as a 'pauper', from the Latin word for poor. On his or her first entry into the workhouse, details of each pauper were written in a register book, standardized for all workhouses. These details included: name, sex, marital status, occupation, religion, physical condition and place of residence. The final column was headed 'date when died or left the workhouse'. Sometimes, not all of these details were filled in. Occasionally, little more than the name and date of entry appears in the register book. Death and birth registers were also kept along with notes of various kinds. Six death registers for the Cork Union, commencing in the year

1853, are to be found in the Cork Archives. These records pre-date the state registration of deaths by eleven years.

The workhouses tried to reduce overcrowding by assisting some of the inmates to emigrate, notably to Australia and the United States. Descendants of Irish emigrants looking for their roots in Ireland might find workhouse register books more productive to their researches than the heraldic records of the Genealogical Office.

The boards of guardians met weekly and kept very good records of their proceedings. The minute books of the Cork Union alone run into 133 large volumes. Although the day-to-day running of the workhouse is the main concern of the minute books, a great deal of local information may be gleaned from them. A recurring theme, especially in the early years, is the difficulty experienced by the guardians in collecting the poor rate. There are many references to appeals against liability to pay rates and prosecutions of defaulters.

Undoubtedly, the records produced directly by the poor law unions are a rich source of genealogical information concerning two classes of Irish people: the destitute, who were inmates, and the wealthy middle class and gentry, who acted in the capacity of guardians. However, we are concerned with the ordinary Irish person, who more than likely was a tenant farmer. Some tenant farmers, in common with some members of all other classes, found themselves among the destitute, due to the disaster of the great famine or some other catastrophe, but as a body, they were affected by the Poor Law because, as occupiers of property, they had to pay for it.

Section 61 of the Poor Law Act states: 'And be it enacted, that for the purpose of defraying the expenses incurred in the Execution of this Act the Guardians of every Union . . . shall, from Time to Time, make and levy such Rates as may be necessary on every Occupier of rateable Heridatements in or arising within such Union.'

The levying of rates in Ireland did not start with the Poor Law. This form of local taxation had been in existence for centuries under the grand juries. The grand jury was an embryonic system of local administration, controlled by landlords and the legal profession. In 1634, the grand juries were enabled by statute to 'tax and set every inhabitant to such reasonable aid and sum of money as they shall think fit by their discretion convenient'.

It is not clear on what basis the assessment was made. Before the year 1826 there is no record of any systematic valuation, but in that year an Act was passed which provided for making a uniform valuation of the several baronies, parishes and other divisions of each county of Ireland. This valuation was to proceed as the Ordnance Survey of any county or division of a county was completed. It was carried out under the supervision of Richard Griffith and was known variously as the 'Townland', 'Government' or 'Ordnance Valuation'. The purpose of the 1826 Act and a later amending Act passed in 1836 was to ensure that the relative values of townlands in different counties, though ascertained at different periods, should be the same. Rateable property was to be valued collectively in each townland and no individual assessments were to be made. Local applotters were to determine the proportion of the rate each occupier of the townland was to pay.

The Poor Law Act authorized a distinct valuation involving individual assessment. This valuation was to be the responsibility of each poor law union. Each board of guardians appointed its own valuers. By 1842 the Poor Law valuation had been completed. The county rate was collected on the basis of the townland valuation and the poor rate was collected on the basis of the Poor Law valuation.

Two distinct valuations were therefore in existence. In 1844 an enquiry was instituted to examine the resulting confusion. The enquiry committee recommended that there should be only one valuation for all purposes of local taxation.

Legislation followed in 1846 and 1852 which authorized one uniform valuation of Ireland according to holdings and based on the principle of net annual value. The work on this new tenement valuation actually started earlier, in 1844, when the Lord Lieutenant instructed Richard Griffith, Commissioner of Valuation, to value individual tenements, 'no matter how minute'. Sir Richard Griffith was so closely identified with this new tenement valuation that it became known as 'Griffith's valuation'.

Valuers attempted to calculate the net annual value of every holding. Buildings were valued by assessing the annual letting value and subtracting all necessary outgoings from that sum, such as cost of insurance, maintenance and repairs. Agricultural land was valued by working out the value of the agricultural produce the land was capable of yielding in a year. This was to be achieved by reference to a fixed scale of prices for certain agricultural products, specified within the 1852 Act. All local circumstances such as aspect, elevation, ease of communication and distance from market towns were to be taken into account. The valuer was to pay particular attention to the quality of the soil and subsoil, since Griffith considered this to be of great importance in determining the capability of land for crop production. The valuer then made allowances for the production costs, taxation level and other outgoings and by subtraction arrived at the net annual value of the tenement.

The valuers worked in groups of three, consisting of a baronial valuer and two assistant valuers. They were accompanied by spadesmen who dug up the surface of the land to facilitate a geological examination of the soil. There was no mountain too barren and no field too remote to visit and so detailed was their examination that there was scarcely any holding of land which they valued at a uniform price.

The work was completed in 1865. Both the townland valuation and the Poor Law valuation were scrapped, and Griffith's valuation became the basis for all local taxation, including the county rate and the poor law rate. It also became the basis of the franchise in parliamentary and local elections and was officially invoked in a variety of situations as disparate as the assessment of compensation for evicted tenants and the calculation of standing electricity charges.

An action brought on behalf of 1800 farmers challenging the constitutionality of the valuation acts reached the High Court in July 1982. Justice Barrington ruling in the case declared the acts to be unconstitutional, thus ending a history of over 130 years.

I have gone into detail about the history of rates because the archive created by Griffith's valuation is probably the richest source of genealogical information in nineteenth-century Ireland. The material divides conveniently into three sections.

First, there are the notebooks of the original valuers, giving various details concerning the quality of the soil, the dimensions of the buildings and the tenure of the occupants. Secondly, the valuation itself when completed was printed by the government. The entire collection consists of more than 200 volumes. Thirdly, there are the 'cancelled books', which record all changes in the ownership and tenure of Irish land from the time of the original valuation right up to the present. Taken as a whole, the documents associated with Griffith's valuation constitute an individual history of every holding in Ireland from the late 1840s up to the present.

The valuers' notebooks are the earliest documents compiled in connection with Griffith's valuation. They are of three types: field books, house books, and tenure books. The pages of the notebooks are divided into columns with printed headings. The first column is for map references, the second column gives the names of the occupiers. In the field books the remaining columns give information about the amount and quality of the land held. The house books are more interesting as they give detailed measurements of the dwellings of the occupiers and the outbuildings they possessed. The tenure books are the most interesting of the three. They give the annual rent paid by each tenant. Valuable information appears in the column headed 'Tenure and Year Let', which normally states whether the tenant had a lease or held the land 'at will', that is, on the sufferance of the landlord from year to year. The date and duration of the lease are also given.

The books covering the Twenty-Six Counties are to be found in the National Archives; those pertaining to Northern Ireland are in the Public Record Office of Northern Ireland. They are arranged by county, barony, civil parish and townland, as indeed are the other two parts of the valuation. Indexes in book form in the reading room make it easy to locate whatever books you are interested in.

The printed version of Griffith's valuation was based on the valuers' notebooks. It did not, however, utilize all the information to be found there, and some of the entries in this slightly later work have been updated. County and city libraries will normally have the volumes appropriate to their localities. The National Library, Kildare Street, Dublin and some other institutions have full collections.

Each page of *Griffith's Valuation* follows the same tabular pattern (see Figure 4). Column one lists map references which are keyed to six inch to the mile Ordnance Survey maps in the possession of the Valuation Office, 6 Ely Place, Dublin, on which the holdings are outlined. Photocopies of these maps may be ordered from the Valuation Office. Column two gives the name of the occupier and therefore is the column of most interest to the researcher. The third column names the landlord or the 'Immediate lessors'. The next column is headed 'Description of Tenement': a typical description of a tenant farmer's holding would be the succinct phrase 'house, offices and land'. The final four columns give the area of land held, the valuation of the land, the valuation of the buildings and the total valuation of the holding.

Finding an entry in *Griffith's Valuation* is very easy. If you know the name of the townland in which the subject of your search lived, the *Alphabetical Index to the Townlands and Towns of Ireland* will give you the name of the civil parish and barony in which it is situated. If you do not know the name of the townland you could try the National Library's typed indexes: 'The Primary Valuation and Tithe Applotment Index of Surnames'. Though this has never been published, it is available in many libraries in typescript form or microfilm.

This work consists of a series of indexes of progressively smaller divisions. There is a general alphabetical index for the whole country, one for each county, and one for each barony. The indexes dealing with divisions of counties are bound in the same volume as the county index. The county index lists alphabetically all the surnames that appear in *Griffith's Valuation* for that county, provided the bearer of the surname is shown as the occupier of a house. The letter 'G', a number, and the name of one or more baronies appear after each surname. The name of the barony or baronies indicate the part or parts of the county in which the surname appears, the number indicates the number of times it appears and the letter 'G' stands for *Griffith's Valuation*. Having narrowed down the name to a particular barony, the index of the barony can be consulted and a

VALUATION OF TENEMENTS.

PARISH OF KILCROHANE.

No. and Letters of Reference to Map.	Townlands and Occupiers.	Immediate Lessors.	Description of Tenement.	Area. A. R. P.	Rateable Annual Valuation. Land. £ s. d.	Buildings. £ s. d.	Total Annual Valuation of Rateable Property. £ s. d.
	BALLYEIRAGH— *continued.*						
6 A	Thaddeus Carty, / Charles Carty, .	Richard Tobin, .	Land, . . .	2 3 20	1 4 0 / 0 12 0	—	1 4 0 / 0 12 0
— B	Thaddeus Carty, / Charles Carty, .	Same, .	Land, . . .	8 3 26	1 8 0 / 0 14 0	—	1 8 0 / 0 14 0
— C	Thaddeus Carty, / Charles Carty, .	Same, .	Land, . . .	1 1 25	0 2 0 / 0 1 0	—	0 2 0 / 0 1 0
— D	Thaddeus Carty, / Charles Carty, .	Same, .	Land, . . .	1 1 10	0 8 0 / 0 4 0	—	0 8 0 / 0 4 0
— E	Thaddeus Carty, / Charles Carty, .	Same, .	Land, . . .	0 2 10	0 4 0 / 0 2 0	—	0 4 0 / 0 2 0
7 a	Richard Tobin, .	Rev. William Evanson,	Offices and land, .	42 3 7	12 13 0	0 10 0	13 3 0
.. b	Owen Carthy, .	Richard Tobin, .	House, . .	—	—	0 5 0	0 5 0
			Total, .	578 2 11	62 8 0	6 18 0	69 6 0
	BALLYNATRA. (*Ord. S.* 138.)						
1	Richard Tobin, .	John B. Gumbleton, .	Land, . . .	20 1 1	6 10 0	—	6 10 0
— a	Ellen Daly, .	Richard Tobin, .	House, . .	—	—	0 5 0	0 5 0
2 a	James Hickey, .	John B. Gumbleton, .	House, offices, and land,	19 0 22	8 0 0	1 10 0	9 10 0
— b	James Donovan, .	James Hickey, . .	House, . .	—	—	0 5 0	0 5 0
			Total, .	39 1 23	14 10 0	2 0 0	16 10 0
	BALLYROON. (*Ord. S.* 138.)						
1	Lawrence Donovan, / Thomas Allen, . / John Coghlan, . / Richard Tobin, . / William Tobin, . / John Tobin, . / Timothy Sullivan,	J. B. Gumbleton, .	Land (*mountain*), .	58 0 9	0 8 0 / 0 2 0 / 0 2 0 / 0 2 0 / 0 2 0 / 0 2 0 / 0 2 0	— / — / — / — / — / — / —	0 8 0 / 0 2 0 / 0 2 0 / 0 2 0 / 0 2 0 / 0 2 0 / 0 2 0
2 a	Timothy Sullivan, .	Same, .	House, office, and land,	9 2 24	5 5 0	0 5 0	5 10 0
— b	Anne Houlihan, .	Same, .	House, . .	—	—	0 2 0	0 2 0
3 A a	William Tobin, / Richard Tobin, / John Coghlan, .	Same, .	House and land, / Land, . . / Land, . .	5 1 26	1 4 0 / 1 4 0 / 1 4 0	0 4 0 / — / —	1 8 0 / 1 4 0 / 1 4 0
— B	William Tobin, / Richard Tobin, / John Coghlan, .	Same, .	Land, . . .	3 2 21	0 12 0 / 0 12 0 / 0 12 0	—	0 12 0 / 0 12 0 / 0 12 0
A b	John Tobin and James Tobin, .	Same, .	House, . .	—	—	0 5 0	0 5 0
4	John Coghlan, / John Tobin, . / James Tobin, .	Same, .	Land, . . .	9 2 30	2 14 0 / 1 7 0 / 1 7 0	—	2 14 0 / 1 7 0 / 1 7 0
— a	Richard Tobin and John Coghlan, .	Same, .	House and office, .	—	—	1 0 0	1 0 0
5 a / b	Laurence Donovan, / Thomas Allen, .	Same, .	House, offices, & land, / House and land,	28 3 35	12 0 0 / 2 8 0	0 10 0 / 0 5 0	12 10 0 / 2 13 0
.. c	Unoccupied, .	Laurence Donovan, .	House, . .	—	—	0 5 0	0 5 0
			Total, .	115 1 25	31 9 0	2 16 0	34 5 0
	BALLYROON MOUNTAIN. (*Ord. S.* 138.)						
1	Laurence Donovan, / Thomas Allen, . / John Coghlan, . / Richard Tobin, . / John Tobin, . / Timothy Sullivan, / William Tobin, .	John B. Gumbleton, .	Land (*mountain*), .	336 1 32	5 5 0 / 1 0 0 / 2 10 0 / 1 5 0 / 1 5 0 / 2 10 0 / 1 5 0	— / — / — / — / — / — / —	5 5 0 / 1 0 0 / 2 10 0 / 1 5 0 / 1 5 0 / 2 10 0 / 1 5 0
— a	Owen Sullivan, .	Richard Tobin, .	House, . .	—	—	0 5 0	0 5 0
2 a	William Conkly, .	John B. Gumbleton, .	House and land, .	2 2 0	0 8 0	0 2 0	0 10 0
3 a	James Tobin, (*Reagh*),	Same, .	House, offices, and land,	127 3 5	7 5 0	0 10 0	7 15 0
			Total, .	466 2 37	22 13 0	0 17 0	23 10 0

Figure 4: *Griffith's Valuation*, County of Cork, Barony of Carbery West, Parish of Kilcrohane

procedure similar to that found in the county index leads to a civil parish. The name is finally located by checking all the surnames in that parish in the appropriate volume of *Griffith's Valuation*. It should be clear that the 'Names Index' is useful only for the relatively rare surnames.

A new and far more helpful index to *Griffith's Valuation* was published in microfiche form in 1987, by All-Ireland Heritage Inc. It is a county-by-county alphabetical index of all occupiers of land which had any type of housing on it. It differs from the National Library indexes in a number of important respects. The names on the index are reproduced exactly as they appear in *Griffith's Valuation*. Apart from giving the Christian name, middle initial(s) and title(s), each entry also gives the relevant civil parish, townland, ordnance survey sheet number, and *Griffith's Valuation* page number. If you find it necessary to consult an index to *Griffith's Valuation*, the All-Ireland Heritage Inc. index is a most useful resource that can save hours of tedium.

Griffith's Valuation, that is, the published version of the survey, reflects the tenure of Irish land as it was in the middle of the last century. As time passed the situation changed. The old proprietors died off or left and were replaced by others. The valuation office kept an account of all these changes by keeping manuscript copies of the original valuation and constantly updating them. The pages of these books, apart from having an extra column, headed 'observations', are identical in appearance to the pages of *Griffith's Valuation*. When a landholder was replaced, a line was drawn through the original holder's name, the name of his replacement was written above it and the year of the change was written in the 'Observations' column. Coloured ink was used for these purposes, so the date of each change could be seen at a glance.

After about fifteen years, an accumulation of changes in inks of different colours gave these books a cramped and confusing appearance. At this point, the procedure was to transcribe the most up-to-date information into a new book, where the same process was continued. Each area required about half a dozen books to accommodate all the changes that took place before the present century began. The old or 'cancelled' books for each individual district were kept together and bound in volumes. They are available for inspection in the Valuation Office, Ely Place, for the twenty-six counties of the Republic. The cancelled books for the Northern Ireland are held at the Public Record Office of Northern Ireland, 66 Balmoral Avenue, Belfast, where they may be inspected free of charge.

Photocopies of the pages that deal with the holding you are interested in may be ordered. They are not very satisfactory because, as already pointed out, dates of changes were indicated by means of coloured ink. When the name of a landholder was crossed out, let's say in green, the name of the new landholder and the date in the 'Observations' column would also be written in green. Four or five colours could be used to indicate changes in a single holding. It is not possible to match changes with dates using a monochrome photocopy.

On the other hand, personal inspection of the books for the Twenty-Six Counties can be rather expensive. People engaged in genealogical research are charged at the rate of £6 per hour. However, the staff of the Valuation Office, Ely Place, provide a very good service. The staff in the front office will usually try to give the visitor some explanation of the records he has come to inspect. The visitor is then conducted to the record store, where more help is available if required.

If you have the name or names of the persons you are interested in, and the townland, parish and barony in which they lived, the appropriate volumes will be presented to you to inspect. Each volume is made up of a number of 'cancelled books', which are arranged in reverse chronological order. You have to go to the last section of the volume, therefore, to find the oldest book. If you bring along some sheets of paper divided into columns corresponding to those in *Griffith's Valuation*, with the addition of a column headed 'Observations', you will be able to copy down the entries as they appear in the books. You should also equip yourself with a minimum of four coloured biros so that you can take down the changes exactly as they appear in the cancelled books. This is a better approach than attempting to interpret and draw conclusions from the information there and then. Once you have everything taken down, you can examine it at your leisure later.

A few general remarks should suffice to underline the significance of the cancelled books to the family historian. The names of the proprietors of any holding can be traced from the 1850s to the present day. This line of succession most often consists of wives succeeding husbands, sons succeeding fathers, sons succeeding mothers. The succession dates often mark some significant event, such as a death, a marriage, a serious illness, emigration. These leads can then be pursued in other record compilations, such as the registers of births, deaths and marriages.

Reference has been made to valuations earlier than Griffith's, namely the townland valuation and those carried out on behalf of the grand juries and boards of guardians. In one of the minute books of the Cork Board of Guardians there is a reference to a new valuation of the union to be carried out in September 1841. In October of the same year the guardians made five pounds available for making out a second copy of a rate collection book 'to expedite collection'. There is no trace of these books now. Almost nothing of earlier valuations remains in existence. The National Archives has fragments for some few towns but seemingly nothing for the countryside.

VI

TITHE APPLOTMENT BOOKS

Tithes were taxes in kind levied on the produce of the agricultural community for the benefit and upkeep of the Established Church. The Catholic tenant was required by law to pay for the support of a Church he regarded as both heretical and alien, and, understandably, regarded tithes with considerable loathing. Through the first four decades of the nineteenth century, this tax was collected with increasing difficulty. During his emancipation campaign, O'Connell constantly made references to the grievances of the tenantry. After the granting of emancipation in 1829 tithes continued to be collected so resistance was stepped up to take the form of a national campaign.

The first engagement in the tithe war was in Graiguena-managh, County Kilkenny, which had a Catholic population of 4779 and 63 Protestants. Mr MacDonald, the Protestant curate, called upon the parish priest, Fr Doyle, for tithes. Having been refused, he seized the priest's horse. Every Catholic in the area then refused to pay and resistance spread. When the parish priest of Doon, County Limerick, ignored a demand for tithes his cow was seized, and sold under singular circumstances. The government sent to the auction a large force of police backed up by fifty cavalrymen, five companies of Highlanders and two cannons. Four thousand people turned up to watch the proceedings. The outcome was rather anticlimactic, however: the animal was sold to the parish priest's brother. In Knocktopher, also in County Kilkenny, in December 1831 twelve policemen, including their commanding officer, were killed and seventeen injured in a clash with anti-tithe protesters.

The government reacted by making a concerted effort to collect outstanding sums, without much success. After months of violence and bloodshed in 1832, the government managed to collect only £12,000, at a cost of £27,000. About one million pounds remained outstanding.

Rathcormac, County Cork, became a focal point in the tithe war in December 1834, when resistance centred on a widow named Ryan who refused to pay. A fight broke out between a group of local people and the police, backed up by the military. Twelve of the local people were killed and 42 were wounded.

A compromise was reached in 1838 when the tithe was reduced by 25 per cent and converted into a fixed rent charge. Responsibility for payment was transferred from tenant to landlord. The hated tithe proctor and tithe farmer were eliminated. These changes resulted in an enormous improvement in the situation and the tithe ceased to be a popular grievance. It was finally abolished in 1869.

The change in the method of collecting tithes was facilitated by two acts that preceded the change. One allowing for the voluntary substitution of a money payment in place of payment in kind was passed in 1823, and another making such substitution compulsory followed in 1832. These Tithe Commutation Acts allowed for a valuation of the country. Under the earlier Act, each civil parish was to have two commissioners, one appointed by the Established Church, the other elected by the ratepayers of the parish. They could arrange a commutation or substitution either by agreement or by valuation. Land valuations were based on the average price in the parish of wheat and oats during the seven years preceding 1 November 1821. By the Act of 1832, the privilege of making a composition by agreement was removed and a single commissioner for each parish was appointed by the Lord Lieutenant. About half the civil parishes were valued between 1823 and 1830 and the remainder before 1837.

Typically, the pages of the tithe applotment books, as the valuers' notebooks were called, are divided into columns and provide information under the following headings: Tenant's Name, Townland, Area, Valuation, Tithe Payable. Unlike Griffith's valuation, there was no overall supervision by a central authority of the tithe valuation, so the books do not present a uniform appearance. Some are strongly bound volumes, while others are poor-quality copybooks. The quality of the information also varies, some giving far more details than those mentioned above, others giving merely a bald statement of the amount of tithe payable by each holding.

There is evidence to indicate that the tithe applotment books do not give a complete list of householders in each parish. In a study carried out in a County Tyrone parish, about half the men who appear in the Roman Catholic baptismal register as fathers of children do not appear in the tithe applotment book. These omissions are possibly due in some cases to the return of the name of one landholder only, in the case of a subdivided farm, and the non-inclusion of cottiers and the poorest inhabitants of a parish. The omissions are not due to the exclusion of pastureland, which, though previously exempted from tithes, had been included under the 1823 Act.

The tithe applotment books relating to Southern Ireland were transferred to the National Archives in 1944. Copies of those relating to the Six Counties are also held in this repository – the originals for the counties of Down, Derry, Armagh, Antrim, Fermanagh and Tyrone were sent to the Public Record Office of Northern Ireland. An index available in the reading room makes locating any tithe applotment book relevant to your researches very easy. Some local libraries have microfilms of the tithe applotment books of the surrounding parishes. These microfilms are of rather poor quality, but a new, clearer microfiche version has recently come on the market and the larger libraries will probably have this improved version soon.

VII

ESTATE RECORDS

Estate Records, if they survived and can be traced, may prove to be a very good source of information. They offer the best, if not the only, chance of tracing a family into the eighteenth century. Therefore, it is worth going to a lot of trouble to locate them.

The historian James S. Donnelly Jr spent eighteen months in Ireland and England between 1967 and 1969 doing research. During much of this time he tried to locate estate records which were the main historical source for his book *The Land and the People of Nineteenth-Century Cork*. He estimated that there were well in excess of 1000 landed proprietors in Cork during the period with which his book deals. However, he was able to locate and use only 31 sets of estate records. He concluded, as well he might, that Irish estate records have an extremely poor survival rate. From the figures he gave, it would seem that less than 3 per cent of estate records survived. He blamed a number of factors for this: the War of Independence, during which many landlords' houses were burned to the ground by the IRA; waste-paper drives, which cleared the archives of many estate agents and solicitors; the Land Commission, which razed the residences of former landlords without making provision for the preservation of the documents that may have been stored within; and the heavy rates that encouraged the demolition of great houses.

Things are not as bad, however, as they might appear. From my own experience there is a 20 to 25 per cent chance of locating the relevant estate records when researching a family of tenant farmer stock. That is not to say that the records will always have pertinent information. A collection of estate papers may consist mostly of wills, marriage settlements, correspondence, mortgages and other documents that make little or no reference to tenants, but rentals and leases could also form part of it. The unexpectedly high rate of success I experienced in locating estate papers is probably due to two factors. First, the work of the Irish Manuscript Commission has continued over the past twenty years. During this time, they have located and reported on a great number of collections of papers in private hands, in many cases acquiring these collections for the state. Secondly, the records of the larger estates tend to have a greater chance of survival than those of smaller ones. A high proportion of those whom I researched lived on large estates.

It is common to find that the records of a single estate have been broken up and deposited in more than one repository. The family may have donated the papers in their possession to one institution, while papers accumulated in the office of the land agent or solicitor of the family may have been passed on to another.

The condition of estate records varies greatly. At worst they may consist of an unsorted pile of dirty papers stuffed into rusty metal trunks and plastic bags. At the other end of the scale they may have been subjected to scholarly scrutiny, edited and published, as, for example, were the papers of the Kenmare estate.

The first step to take towards locating estate papers is to find the name of the landlord. This may be done by consulting the 'Immediate Lessors' column in *Griffith's Valuation*. The great landlords are more likely to have accumulated papers than those who held only a few hundred acres, so the next step should be to establish the extent of the landlord's holding. A government publication of 1876 lists the landlords of each county alphabetically, giving the address of the owner, the extent of his estate and the valuation. The book has a rather long-winded title: *Copy of a return of the names of the proprietors and the area and valuation of all properties in the several counties in Ireland, held in fee or perpetuity, or on long leases at chief rents, prepared for the use of his majesty's government and printed by Alexander Thom, 87 and 88 Abbey Street, Dublin by the direction of the Irish government and at the expense of the treasury, House of Commons, 1876.*

A more useful book to consult for this information is *The Landowners of Ireland* by U. H. Hussey de Burgh. This gives 'an alphabetical list of the owners of estates of 500 acres or £50 valuation and upwards in Ireland with the acreage and valuation in each county and a brief notice of the education and official appointments of each person, to which are added his town and county addresses and clubs'.

The chief difference between the two books is that whereas the former focuses on the counties, the latter focuses on the landowners. The only way of telling whether the landlord you looked up in the government publication of 1876, say under the heading of 'County Kerry', had estates anywhere else in Ireland is to check each of the other thirty-one counties for his name. Knowing the size of a landholder's estate in one county only can be very misleading. A man with a small estate in one county may have substantial holdings elsewhere. In The Landowners of Ireland, each landowner's name appears once and beneath his name is listed the number of acres he holds in each county. The landlord's name and some knowledge of the extent and location of his holdings allows the search for estate records to begin in earnest. I have found that the following six approaches often led to success.

The Irish Manuscript Commission carried out a programme aimed at surveying all collections of estate papers in private hands whose owners were willing to have them examined. A report was written on each collection. Representative samples of these reports were published in *Analecta Hibernica*, numbers 15, 20 and 25. The entire collection of reports is available for examination at the Genealogical Office, 2 Kildare Street, Dublin. Each report consists of a number of foolscap-size typescript pages, bound in volumes. *Analecta Hibernica* No. 20 contains a names index keyed to the reports. A list of the reports made up to 1965 is given in *Analecta Hibernica* No. 23 and those made since that date are listed in *Analecta Hibernica* No. 32 (1985). If there is a report on the estate papers of the landlord you are researching, his name will appear in one of the lists along with the number of the relevant report.

After the famine the British administration was forced to concede that there was something radically wrong with the system of land tenure in Ireland. Two possible solutions were proposed: give the tenants more security so that they would develop the initiative to improve their holdings without the fear of an increase in rent; or replace the landlords with a more dynamic set with capital to invest. The all-powerful land lobby ensured that the second approach was tried first.

Many Irish landlords were only too willing to sell their land, the problem was that the process of establishing title was difficult, sometimes impossible, and very expensive and time-consuming. The Encumbered Estates Act of 1849 was designed to facilitate the sale of land by establishing an Encumbered Estates Court, which was given power to cut through much of the red tape that had previously held up sales. Between 1849 and 1857 over 3000 Irish estates were sold to approximately 7200 purchasers. The records of the Encumbered Estates court, indexed by landlord's name, may be examined in the National Archives. This material is particularly rich in maps and rentals which were prepared to facilitate prospective buyers.

Richard J. Hayes's *Manuscript Sources for the History of Irish Civilization* is one of the surest ways of locating estate records. The landlords' names should be looked up in the 'people' volumes. Because landlords tended to have titles and unusual surnames, the problem of confusion over common surnames is not as serious as it is with tenants. Hayes gives the name of the repository in which the estate papers are stored and occasionally a brief list of the documents in the collection. Some repositories will supply a full list, from which one can order selected items.

The firm of solicitors that acted for the landlord may still be in business. It may know something about the location of the estate papers or may even have them in its possession. The easiest way of finding out the name of the firm that acted for the landlord is through the Land Commission. The bulk of Irish agricultural land was sold by the landlords, through the Land Commission, to their tenants between 1881 and 1923.

It is sometimes possible to contact the descendants of nineteenth-century landlords, and the modern-day representatives of the family may be able to give information on the location of estate papers. The various editions of *Burke's Landed Gentry of Ireland* and *Debrett's Peerage and Baronetage* can prove very useful in this regard. People with titles are particularly easy to trace forward using those books, as the addresses of the present-day title holders are usually listed.

Local libraries, heritage centres and local archives are worth checking. They may have the records, or the personnel may know where to find them. Local historians may have located estate records in the course of their researches on related subjects. Historical journals usually give sufficient details about the authors of articles to enable readers to contact them.

VIII

WILLS AND ADMINISTRATIONS

When a person dies, his or her property is normally frozen; nobody can buy or sell or deal with it in any way. This is the case even if the deceased left a will, for a will is only a piece of paper and cannot be acted on until it is proved. Probate is the process that legalizes a will. The court appoints an executor under a will or an administrator if there is no will. Only then can the property be apportioned according to the will or to the laws of inheritance, as the case may be.

It is not difficult to imagine the importance of wills as a genealogical source. The last written instructions of a person relating to the disposition to be made of property and minor children promises to be full of the sort of information that amply rewards painstaking research. Writing in 1910, W.P.W. Phillimore stated: 'rarely can any pedigree of more than two or three generations be compiled without reference to them'. This opinion has certainly been borne out by the experience of many researchers who have found themselves stuck around the turn of the nineteenth century – the period to which Mr Phillimore was referring.

There are many reasons why one would expect wills to have a high survival rate: the intrinsic importance of the documents; the process of proving them; the retention of wills by the courts of probate. These expectations, however, are not fulfilled. The story of Irish wills is largely the story of loss upon loss. It is not my intention to relate that story in detail. This work has already been done by Rosemary ffolliott in *Irish Genealogy: A Record Finder*, and I am concerned with testamentary records only insofar as they impinge upon the bulk of the population in the nineteenth century. My outline of Irish wills and administrations is for purposes of orientation. I will also try to assess which testamentary collections are worth examining in more detail.

Up to 1858 the Church of Ireland had jurisdiction over matters of probate. Each diocese had a Consistorial Court where wills were proved. If the deceased had 'bona notabilia', i.e. effects, worth more than five pounds in two or more dioceses, the will would come under the jurisdiction of the Prerogative Court of the Archbishop of Armagh, Primate of Ireland.

The Probate Act of 1857 transferred testamentary jurisdiction from the Church of Ireland to a new Court of Probate. The wills and administrations that had been accumulated by both the Prerogative and Consistorial Courts were eventually transferred to the National Archives, where they were copied into will books. A will index was made for each diocese and the Prerogative wills and administrations were also indexed. A major loss of wills becomes apparent at this point. It is clear that not all wills and administrations that had been processed by Church of Ireland courts were sent to the National Archives. There is no way of calculating the number that went missing. The proportion seems to have varied from one diocese to another. Generally speaking, few wills that pre-date 1780 reached the National Archives.

In place of the ecclesiastical courts, the 1857 legislation established a Principal Registry in Dublin, which took over the function of the Prerogative Court and also covered a wide area around the capital; and eleven District Registries to cover the rest of the country, replacing the Consistorial Courts. A continuous stream of wills and grants of administration flowed from these courts to the National Archives. The great bulk of testamentary material thus gathered was destroyed in the fire of 1922, including almost all of the Prerogative Court records – wills, will books, grants of administration and grant books; most of the records of the Consistorial Courts; almost all the wills and grants of administration from the Principal and District Registries; and most of the transcript will books from the Principal Registry. Indexes to all the collections were saved, though some were damaged.

Since the fire, the National Archives has managed to assemble an impressive collection of wills and will substitutes, and it can again boast the most extensive such collection in Ireland. The most important items are: notebooks of genealogical abstracts of about 37,000 prerogative wills and about 5000 prerogative administrations that had been made from the original documents by Sir William Betham; Irish will registers, 1828-39, and yearly indexes to Irish will registers, 1828-78, obtained from the Commissioners of Inland Revenue, London, which contain references to wills from all courts; a miscellaneous collection of wills and will substitutes – still being added to – which is keyed to a card index in the search room; transcript will books from the eight District Registries that cover the Twenty-Six Counties.

The will books from the remaining three District Registries – Armagh, Belfast and Derry – are held in the Public Record Office of Northern Ireland. That repository has succeeded in accumulating a large collection of wills – not all pertaining exclusively to Northern Ireland – keyed to a card index.

Other institutions also have collections of wills, notably the National Library, the Genealogical Office, the Registry of Deeds and the Land Commission. Much testamentary material has been published in a variety of books and periodicals.

The extent to which the average tenant farmers made wills and the extent to which these wills survived can only be guessed at. Wills are so scattered that it would be impractical to attempt to check every source. A researcher will always have misgivings about anything but a thorough approach, but in this complex area a workmanlike attitude is required of all those who do not wish to make a lifetime study of wills.

First of all, certain collections may be fairly confidently eliminated from a research programme. A tenant farmer's will is highly unlikely to have qualified for the Prerogative Court. Unless he had a leasehold interest in a farm that straddled two dioceses – which is easily ascertained – there is every reason to believe that he would not have fulfilled the condition of possessing property to the value of five pounds or more in two dioceses. It is almost certain that all wills held by the Land Commission are those of landowners and not tenants. Landlords submitted these wills as part of the corroborative evidence of title when they were disposing of their estates under the various Land Purchase Acts. The index to this collection is in the National Library. The wills in the National

Library have not been gathered into a single collection, nor is there a single index covering wills, so research there would be both difficult and slow.

The following testamentary records merit research, both because there is some possibility of finding relevant wills and because research can be carried out quickly and easily: Consistorial will indexes; the alphabetical card index in the National Archives and its counterpart in the Public Record Office of Northern Ireland; the yearly *Calendars to Wills and Administrations*, commencing in 1858; the yearly indexes that came from the Commissioners of Inland Revenue; the Index to the Genealogical Office's will abstracts; and the abstracts of wills in the Registry of Deeds.

The Consistorial will indexes are available for consultation at the National Archives. Some have been published and are available at city and county libraries. Ryan's *Irish Records: Sources for Family and Local History* lists the published indexes under the appropriate county. The published will index for the diocese of Cork, Cloyne and Ross extends over the whole of County Cork. It deals with a period of about 200 years and makes reference to over 6400 wills. However, this represents less than three wills per month for the largest county in Ireland. The index was published in 1910, when all 6400 wills could be seen in the National Archives, so scant information is given in the index itself. The following is a typical entry: 'Edmond Walsh, Dawstown will probated 1794 Cloyne'. Unless the National Archives managed to get a copy of this will since the fire, this is the sum total of information the researcher is left with. If the National Archives had acquired a copy or an abstract of this will, reference would be found in the alphabetical card index to testamentary records, in the search room.

Abstracts of all administrations granted and of all wills probated since 1858 are to be found in year books in the National Archives. These abstracts are fairly detailed, giving the name, address and marital status of the deceased; the dates of death and probate; the names and addresses of the executors; and the value of the assets of the deceased. An index covering the period 1858-77 is available as an aid to checking the year books. This can save time as it enables the researcher to do a quick check on twenty years by examining one book, rather than twenty. As already stated, the District Registry transcript will books are now divided between the National Archives and the Public Record Office of Northern Ireland, so full copies of most of the wills referred to in the year books may be obtained. It should be remembered, however, that most of the transcript will books from the Principal Registry were destroyed in the Four Courts fire along with the original wills.

The Principal Registry and the District Registries established in 1858 still function. Each Principal Registry has a set of the yearly calendars to wills and administrations mentioned above. These records are open to the public on payment of a one pound fee. If you do your research in one of the District Registries and manage to locate a will abstract that you are interested in, you can write to the National Archives for a full copy of the will. These copies are very expensive, however. An initial fee of twenty pounds is charged, plus one pound per page. This is because the pages of will books are not photocopied, as the spines of the books could be damaged in the process, and copies are taken by microfilming. If you visit the National Archives, you can transcribe the will yourself at no cost.

The main collection of will abstracts in the Genealogical office was covered by an index published in *Analecta Hibernica* No. 17 in 1949. Though the collection has been added to since, the bulk of the material is listed in this printed and widely available index.

Wide availability is probably the chief merit – considering the group we are dealing with – of *Registry of Deeds: Abstracts of Wills*, edited by P. B. Eustace and published by the Stationery Office. This three-volume work consists of genealogical abstracts of wills logged in the Registry of Deeds in the eighteenth century. The abstracts are arranged alphabetically and keyed to the records of the Registry so that the full document may be consulted easily.

IX

THE REGISTRY OF DEEDS

The Registry of Deeds was established by an Act of parliament in 1708, which provided for the setting up of a central office in Dublin for the registration of all transactions concerning land, such as conveyances, leases and mortgages.

Deeds were registered by copying them either in their complete form or in the form of substantial abstracts. These copies, known as 'memorials', were stored in vaults in lead-lined boxes. Transcriptions of memorials were written into large heavy books in date order. Each of these 'Abstract and Transcript Books' contains about 600 leaves of parchment – elephant size – with writing on both sides. They require 'the whole strength of the arm to manage so as not to be easily stolen out for fraudulent purpose'. These books and the indexes to them are at the offices of the Registry of Deeds, Henrietta Street, Dublin.

Members of the public have a statutory right, on payment of a fee, to consult the indexes and the abstract and transcript books, to take notes of the contents and, in the presence of an official, to examine any memorial.

There are two indexes to this great mass of material. The 'Names Index' lists the grantors in alphabetical order in volumes covering periods which vary from two to twenty-one years. The earliest volumes of the 'Names Index' cover the period 1708 to 1729.

The 'Land Index' is arranged in volumes by county. Each county is subdivided into its baronies. Townlands which are the subject of registered transactions are listed alphabetically under the barony in which they are situated. Like the 'Names Index', the 'Land Index' does not cover the entire period from 1708 to the present time as a single unit. It is a series of indexes in which consecutive periods are covered. The first section encompasses the first thirty years – 1708 to 1738. Copies of both indexes are available on microfilm at the National Library.

When you locate an entry which interests you, in either index, an index number will lead you to the book in which the memorial has been transcribed.

Margaret Dickson Falley states in *Irish and Scotch-Irish Ancestral Research* that the Registry of Deeds is one of the most certain sources of ancestral information concerning families in a wide range of social stations and material wealth, and that records of tenants in modest circumstances may be found there. The examples she gives, however, relate to Scotch-Irish from Northern Ireland.

The statute that established the Registry of Deeds, five years after the passing of the Penal Code, described its purpose as being: 'for securing purchases, preventing forgeries and fraudulent gifts and conveyances of land, tenements and hereditaments, which have been frequently practised in this kingdom, especially by Papists to the great prejudice of the Protestant interest thereof'.

From 1704 no Catholic could purchase a lease for more than 31 years, nor could any Catholic invest in mortgages. This legislation was not repealed until the 1780s. In many respects the Registry of Deeds was an adjunct to the Penal Code. Although there is general agreement among modern historians of the Catholic Church that the Penal Code was rarely applied in its full rigour, it must have greatly reduced the number of transactions concerning Catholics that were registered in the Registry of Deeds in the first 70 years of its existence.

The landlord class had such ascendancy over their tenants that registration of leases would have been superfluous as a means of guarding its interests, besides which, the tenantry were too repressed and ignorant to insist on such a measure. Registered deeds are made for the most part between economic equals or near-equals, who might contemplate taking legal action against one another. A lease from a great landlord to a small tenant hardly ever reached the registry, though a lease between a small estate-holder and a prosperous tenant might. Small farmers and cottiers rarely figured in registered deeds.

It is impossible to say what percentage of deeds were actually registered. Samplings from private collections indicate that it was only a small portion of those executed, especially in the eighteenth century. That is not to say that registered deeds are few in number. Over half a million were deposited up to 1832, and at present there are over three million deeds in that repository.

The tenure books associated with Griffith's valuation are a useful starting-point for anyone who contemplates doing a search in the Registry of Deeds. These books show whether a tenant was a tenant-at-will, in which case there is no point in searching, or whether he held a lease, in which case the year of the lease is indicated. If the lease was registered and found, it could lead to earlier leases and a great mine of information. It is likely, however, that most leases executed between landlord and tenant were simply retained with the landlord's collection of estate papers.

How important then is the Registry of Deeds as a source of information concerning the ordinary Catholic tenant farmer? My own experience makes me sceptical of its value. However, a definitive assessment of such a huge archive would require numerous samplings spread over a wide geographical area and covering the first two hundred years or so of its long history. Pending such a study, judgment must be suspended.

X

THE RELIGIOUS CENSUS OF 1766

On 5 March 1766 the following resolution was passed by the Irish House of Lords:

Resolved, that the several archbishops and bishops of this Kingdom shall be and are hereby desired to direct the parish ministers in their respective dioceses to return a list of the several families in their parishes to the House on the first Monday after the recess, distinguishing which are Protestants and which are Papists, as also a list of the several reputed Popish priests and friars residing in their parishes.

Neither the House of Lords nor the prelates laid down rules as to the amount of detail to be collected, nor the manner in which the information was to be presented. Consequently, the quality of these surveys varies enormously from parish to parish. The best returns list householders by name under the townlands within the parish, giving the number of persons of each religion in each household. Less satisfactory returns list householders within the parish, stating their religion but not disclosing the townlands in which they resided. Some returns simply state the numbers of Catholics and Protestants residing in the parish.

Most of the returns were made in March and April 1766. When received by the House of Lords they were arranged in alphabetical order within each diocese and stamped with a running number. The returns eventually ended up in the National Archives, where they suffered a fate similar to many other documents in that repository: apart from some of the returns for the dioceses of Armagh, Cashel and Emly, Cork and Ross, and Waterford, all the original documents were destroyed.

A great deal of copying had taken place before the fire. There is an index to the surviving material, both original and copied, in the reading room of the National Archives, called: 'Religious Census of 1766, A Guide to the Surviving Material'. It includes transcripts of returns held by the Public Record Office of Northern Ireland, the National Library, the Genealogical Office and Trinity College, Dublin. The dioceses for which material survives are listed alphabetically. A page number after the name of each diocese leads to a list of parishes for which material survives, either in its original form or in replacement copies.

Between the Religious Census and the tithe applotment books, the next source of information that is likely to be available, there is a gap of about sixty years. Unless one can find a will, estate records or something else to bridge this gap, the information in the Religious Census is often rendered useless.

XI

HEARTH MONEY ROLLS

An Act of 1662 introduced the Hearth Tax to Ireland:

From and after the twenty-ninth day of September, in the year of our Lord God one thousand six hundred sixty two, every dwelling and other house and edifice that are or hereafter shall be erected within this kingdom of Ireland, other than such as in this Act are hereinafter excepted, shall be chargeable, and by this present Act be and are charged with the annual payment to the King's majesty, his heirs and successors for every fire hearth, and other place used for firing and stoves within every such house and edifice as aforesaid, the sum of two shillings, sterl. by the year, to be paid yearly and every year at the feast of the annunciation of the Blessed Virgin St Mary, and the feast of St Michael the Archangel, by even and equal portions.

The tax was to be paid by the tenant in every house rather than by the landlord. Poor widows and those who could not get their living by work were exempted. Those liable to pay were entered in lists according to the county, barony, parish and townland in which they lived. These lists are known as 'Hearth Money Rolls'. The tax continued to be collected until after the Act of Union of 1800.

The hearth money collectors' returns of the number of houses in the country have been used as the most accurate available means of calculating the population of Ireland in the pre-census period. The method involved taking the number of houses returned in the year under consideration, and multiplying it by an estimate of the average number of people per house. These calculations are based on the assumption that almost all houses were included in the returns. If this is true, it means that hearth money rolls are virtually a list of householders in Ireland in the mid-seventeenth century.

In his book *The Population of Ireland 1750-1845*, K. H. Connell provides a great deal of evidence to show that this assumption is incorrect. He points out, quoting contemporary sources, that collectors were often too lazy to go into districts that were hostile or difficult of access. They also tended to keep for themselves some of the taxes they collected. Therefore, they returned lower numbers of houses than in reality existed. The hearth money collectors' returns for the year 1712 indicate that there were less than 350,000 houses in Ireland. K. H. Connell estimates (though his figures have been questioned lately) that the real number was as high as 525,000, which would suggest that only about two-thirds of the householders were written into the rolls.

None of the original rolls survives. They too were destroyed in the fire of 1922. Copies exist for some areas. Edward MacLysaght lists these and where they may be found in *Seventeenth Century Hearth Money Rolls*. They are all dated 1662-69.

Even if a copy of the hearth money roll exists for a particular area, it is likely to be of little value to the family historian. The gap of one hundred years between the hearth money rolls and the next general survey of the country, the Religious Census of 1766, is far too great to allow a positive connection to be made between a person named in the earlier and a person named in the later list. The surveys are separated by three generations.

XII

RECORDS OF THE GRAVEYARD

Records of the graveyard divide into three categories: gravestone inscriptions, transcriptions of gravestone inscriptions, and cemetery registry books. Of these, the register books are the most informative and the most rare. They are a modern development and are associated with the large municipal cemeteries only. Since it opened in 1869, St Finbarr's Cemetery in Cork kept a most sophisticated system of cross-referenced registers. These books enable the superintendent, without difficulty, to list all those buried in any particular grave, to locate the grave of anyone buried in the cemetery – provided the name and approximate date of interment is known – and to give the following details concerning any person buried in the cemetery: name, date of death, cause of death, sex, religion, age, occupation, place of birth, last place of residence, marital status, date of interment, name of informant.

This service renders gravestones unnecessary. Some of the old cemeteries in the countryside have started to keep written records. They do not go back very far, however, and are not as elaborate. Records of burials in St Gobnait's Cemetery, Ballyvourney, County Cork, for example, didn't begin until 1950, when a new portion of the cemetery was opened.

Much work has been done in transcribing and publishing gravestone inscriptions. Unfortunately, the quality of this work varies. While some surveys are both accurate and comprehensive, this appears to be the exception rather than the rule. Mr R. Henchion is the author of a series of articles on the gravestone inscriptions of County Cork published in the *Journal of the Cork Historical and Archaeological Society*. In the first article referring to gravestone transcriptions, he states: 'Records are invariably incomplete and unbelievably inaccurate. In the *Journal of the Society for the Preservation of the Memorials of the Dead*, there are numerous transcriptions of Co. Cork gravestone inscriptions but their value is completely negatived by repeated errors in dates, personal names and townland titles. In 1965 the transcriptions from Aghinagh were first published but out of a possible 87 inscriptions to be found in the graveyard, only 66 were reproduced in any degree of completeness – those omitted being the oldest and, consequently, the most important – and a mere 23 were free of error.'

Finding out whether a particular graveyard has been surveyed and locating the gravestone transcriptions may also prove to be difficult. The Association for the Preservation of the Memorials of the Dead started publishing its journal in 1888. Thirteen volumes were produced altogether. There is the very impressive, 19-volume collection entitled *Gravestone Inscriptions, County Down*, for those doing genealogical research in that part of the country. Local historical journals are a sure source of this kind of material. *Irish Genealogy: A Record Finder* provides a county-by-county list of gravestone inscriptions recorded in printed sources.

On the positive side it can be said of gravestones that they have proved to be remarkably durable. Two surveys carried out in Kilcrea Abbey, County Cork – one in 1909 and the other in 1967 – indicated that the number and condition of the gravestones had not changed in the intervening six decades. It is usually possible therefore to check the accuracy of transcriptions.

The standard practice these days is for a deceased person to be buried in a family grave, one or two plots wide. If a headstone is erected, the name, address, date of death and occasionally the age of the deceased is carved into it. There is an understandable tendency to assume that this is what was done from time immemorial. In Ireland, however, the general use of this type of family grave is of relatively recent origin. The practice crept into cities and large towns in the 1850s and spread to the countryside around the turn of the century.

The previous practice was a kind of communal burial, which is possibly the last remnant of the old Gaelic sept system. Those bearing a common surname within a parish would have a large section, perhaps eight plots wide, in the parish cemetery. All members of this very extended family would be buried in this large plot. The exact position in which a person was placed in a communal grave of this kind had less to do with the position of a previously interred spouse or child than with the efficient use of the ground.

The Christian understanding of the Day of Judgment had a strong influence on burial practices. Those who could afford to do so kept their bodies intact so that they could rise without impediment on the last day. For this reason entombment within the vaults of a church was the ideal. The majority had to make do with burial in the churchyard. The south side, with its associations of light, was preferred as a site for a grave. The north side was always avoided. Graves normally had, and still have, an east-west alignment, so that when Christ appears in the east and the dead are resurrected they will be facing their judge.

The coffin, as a means of keeping a body intact, is purely symbolic. About thirty-five years after a burial, the remains practically cease to exist. The body has merged with the earth.

The modern single plot grave is capable of taking about four coffins, even if the burials take place within a few years of one another. If the burials are spread over a longer period, more coffins can be accommodated. About a dozen people could be buried in a single plot grave in the course of a century. The large plots in the old country cemeteries could take up to a hundred people in the same period, and many have been in use for hundreds of years.

It would appear that Catholics were more inclined to erect gravestones than were Protestants. In a very informative article in *The Irish Ancestor* (vol. x, no. l, pp. 18-23) Rosemary ffolliott states that whereas Protestants did not consider gravestones to be of any great importance, many a Catholic small farmer set up a monument to his wife or parents.

Gravestones must be looked at in this context. Several hundred people may be buried in one of these large graves. An old stone is likely to refer to only one or two of those interred. It is not reasonable, therefore, to assume that the names on the headstone are in your direct line. Nor does the date on the headstone mark the year that burials began. Interment on that spot could have been taking place for half a millennium before the stone was set up.

Modern headstones – those dated after the middle of the last century – signify a division of the communal plot into genuine family plots. Unfortunately, the headstone inscription that details several generations or that gives a biography of the deceased is a rarity among the class with which this study deals. Going along to an old graveyard in the hope that you'll find a relevant inscription is normally a waste of time, unless you have some evidence of the fact that it was the burial place of the family you are researching. Knowing the location within the graveyard of that family's place of burial is also almost essential. Even then, you'll probably learn nothing and may as well enjoy the irony of learning so little while being as close as possible to your ancestors.

4

USING THE SOURCES

In this section I give an outline of my own family tree to illustrate the methods of research I used in constructing it, and to define more clearly how successful one may expect to be. To avoid tedious repetition, it is assumed that previous sections have been read.

Doing a family tree can be a once-in-a-lifetime chore or a lifelong hobby. The method of research suggested here will suit either approach. It involves four separate stages, at the end of which the chore should be respectably completed or the hobby given an excellent start.

When I started my researches, I considered it wise to do my children's family tree rather than my own, thus including my wife's ancestors. As well as being conducive to domestic harmony, this approach offers greater prospects of success. A basic assumption in this kind of genealogical research is that the families being researched occupied the townlands wherein the family farms lay for many generations. Up to relatively recent times, people found their marriage partners very close to home. As a result of this, one can find all one's researches concentrated in one or two baronies or even parishes, in which the records may be poor. The inclusion of a spouse's family usually helps to avoid this possibility.

Most people are familiar with the way the traditional family tree is drawn. The names are written in horizontal rows, one beneath the other. Each row represents a different generation, the topmost being the earliest. Lines and symbols are used to indicate relationships.

The more comprehensive approach to family history suggested here requires a different type of diagrammatic representation. A series of seven concentric circles is drawn. You write your own name in the innermost circle. Moving outwards, you bisect the space in between the first and second circles and write one of your parents' names in each half. The next space is quartered and a grandparent's name is written in each quarter. Continue with this process until you reach the outermost space, divided into 64 segments for the names of your 64 great, great, great, great, grandparents (see Figure 5).

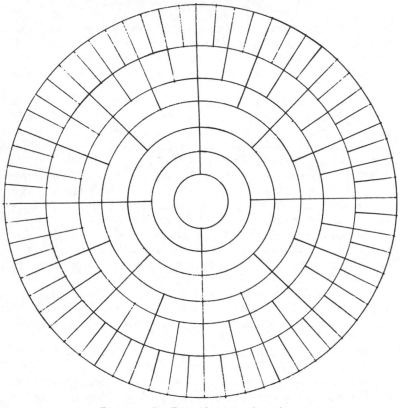

Figure 5: Family circle chart

This configuration has many attractions. Its circular nature, like King Arthur's table, avoids ascribing special importance to any individual or group of ancestors. They are all equal. It is also satisfyingly egocentric. It suggests that the purpose in life of each one of your ancestors was to play his or her part in your creation. The figure is reminiscent of the ripples created when a stone drops into still water. As they move further from the centre, the ripples become wider and weaker, just as ancestors become more numerous and more remote in the outer circles. The idea of a genetic pool which it brings to mind has a more pleasing hold on the imagination than does the idea of a family tree.

One hundred and twenty ancestors fit into the seven-circle configuration, excluding the parents and grandparents in the innermost sections, to whom the term 'ancestors' is not normally applied. The object of the family historian is to collect as much information as possible about each one of these individuals and afterwards to render this information into interesting forms, such as charts, biographies and maps.

This information will come in various forms: books, magazines, newspaper cuttings, letters, certificates, first-hand accounts of witnesses, photographs, photocopies, transcriptions from various archives, abstractions from books and archives, notes on successful and unsuccessful searches. The family historian must cope with a miscellany of information about many different people. Two other factors complicate things: the brothers and sisters and the first, second and even third cousins of ancestors often have to be investigated, to aid identification of earlier generations. Secondly, research usually proceeds in short bouts, spread over a long period.

The information gathered, therefore, must be indexed so that all facts relating to each individual may be located easily. It is impractical to open a separate file for each individual. Much of the material that one is likely to gather will relate to several ancestors. A birth certificate, for instance, will give the name of the child, but also the mother's maiden name, the father's name and his occupation. The certificate cannot be physically placed in three files simultaneously. A method of storing and indexing information which I found satisfactory is described in chapter 6.

STAGE I

The first stage of research involved gathering as much information as possible from the living. I wrote down the names of grandparents and great-grandparents, dates of birth, marriage and death, names of the townlands in which the people lived – the solid stuff from which pedigrees are made.

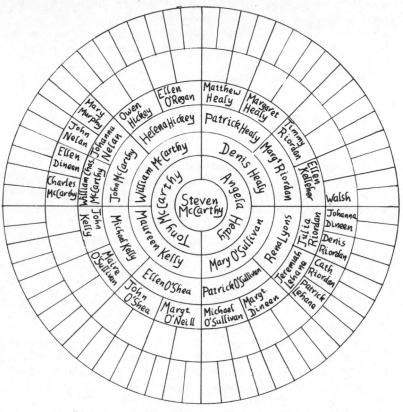

Figure 6: Stage I family circle chart

I was particularly interested in finding out the pre-marriage addresses of the women. It is difficult and sometimes impossible to gain this information from any source but the living. It is important because weddings took place and were registered in the home parish of the bride. I also noted down the less substantial material: family traditions and conjecture; vague and uncertain recollections. Such information, in combination with facts turned up by later research, can prove very useful.

Using this information, I constructed a preliminary family circle (Figure 6). The chart confirms the notion that, apart from knowing something about their grandparents, people in general have no knowledge of their ancestors. Most of the information came from the third generation on the chart, my father's generation, so the fourth and fifth generations, representing the parents and grandparents of the third generation, are complete. Only Patrick Healy's mother's maiden name is missing. The fact that this man died at the age of 41, at a time when his children were all under 12 years of age, explains the absence of this information.

It was possible to get the names of eight of the 32 people in the sixth generation. Six of these names came directly and two indirectly from people of the fourth generation. Again, people were simply naming their grandparents. The surname 'Walsh' – no Christian name – was the only example I came across of someone being able to name a great-grandparent.

STAGE II

Eventually I reached a point at which no more progress could be made without consulting written records. The very appearance of the family circle suggested a procedure: fill in as many blanks in the sixth generation as can be done without too much difficulty. It is best to avoid an obsession to fill in all 32 spaces at this stage and to concentrate on gathering the greatest number of names for the least effort. Apart from producing a more symmetrical chart, this approach, I felt, would increase the spread of names and townlands, thus giving later researches greater prospects of success. A second objective I had at this point was to establish important dates, such as births, marriages, deaths, inheritance and migration, as accurately as possible. I managed to add 13 names without much difficulty (see Figure 7), always following the rule of working from the known to the unknown.

I started with my wife's grandfather, Patrick Healy. I knew from Stage I research that he died in the South Infirmary, Cork, in 1913. The name, place of death, and year of death were sufficient to get a death certificate, which gave his age – 33 years, and exact date of death – 8 January. Using this date I was able to find his entry in the very comprehensive burial records of St Finbarr's Cemetery. Among other things, it gave Ballyvourney as his place of birth.

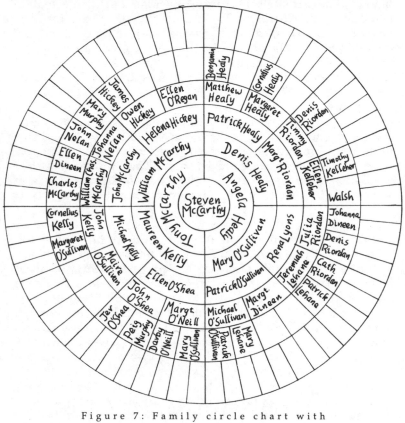

Figure 7: Family circle chart with
names added at Stage II

Ballyvourney is situated in the Registrar's District of Slieveragh, Macroom, County Cork. I was able to examine the birth registers for this district personally at the Births, Deaths and Marriages Registration Office, 18 Liberty Street, Cork. The facts known to me about Patrick Healy at the time, from my Stage I research, were that he had a brother, Daniel, who went to the USA and predeceased him; his father was Matthew Healy and his mother was Margaret; Matthew was probably a publican. On the basis of his age on the death certificate, Patrick Healy should have been born around 1879. However, the only Patrick Healy born in the Slieveragh district between 1864 and 1893 who came anywhere near fitting all the facts was born on St Patrick's Day 1871. His father was Matthew and his mother was Margaret Healy, formerly Healy. Further research in the birth registers confirmed that this indeed was the Patrick Healy that I was looking for – on 20 April 1869 a Daniel Healy was born to the same parents. I then checked the marriage register for the same district and after only a few minutes I discovered the marriage entry of Matthew Healy and Margaret Healy. This gave me the date of the wedding, 26 February 1867, and the names of the bride's and groom's fathers, Cornelius Healy and Ben Healy respectively. An extra bonus was that the ages of the bride and groom were also given. Matthew was 26 years old and Margaret was 27. It is more normal to find the phrase 'full age' for both parties in a marriage register.

The names Denis Riordan and Timmy Kelleher were taken from the marriage certificate of Timmy Riordan and Ellen Kelleher. I had some difficulty locating this marriage entry. Neither the Cork nor Mallow office was able to furnish it, so I sent the details, insofar as I knew them, to the central office of the Registrar General: Joyce House, 8/11, Lombard Street East, Dublin 2. I received the certificate after a three-week wait.

The name 'Patrick Sullivan' was taken from *Griffith's Valuation*. From Stage I research I knew that the Sullivan farm was in the townland of Gortnascarty. The Ballyvourney parish records are available in printed form in *O'Kief Coshe Mang*. I was able to locate the baptismal entry of Michael O'Sullivan and found from this that his mother's name was Mary Lehane.

A book entitled *Who Were my Ancestors? Genealogy (Family Trees) of the Eyeries Parish, Castletownbere, Co. Cork, Ireland* gave me the names in the quarter of the chart dealing with my mother's family. This book gives a tremendous amount of information concerning the people of the parish. It would have been possible to get the information from original sources, but having access to it in this form saved a great deal of time, effort and, indeed, money, as the cost of searches and certificates in Civil Registration records mounts up.

The name 'James Hickey' was located in *Griffith's Valuation*. Knowing that the Hickeys' farm was situated in the townland of Ballynatra, I was able by reference to the *Townland Index* to find out that it was in the civil parish of Kilcrohane and the barony of Carbery. This information enabled me to locate Ballynatra in *Griffith's Valuation*. The only Hickey in the list of occupiers of that townland was James Hickey.

STAGE III

When I had the family circle reasonably complete to the sixth generation, the next phase of research seemed to suggest itself: select lines for more intensive research. Over a long period it is likely that most lines may be pushed back, but in case interest wanes, it is best to get as much as possible out of the time, effort and money invested.

To facilitate this selection process, I drew up two charts. The first chart (Figure 8) provides information essential to further research. It attempts to establish each person of the sixth generation within eight important administrative divisions. The name of the townland is the key to establishing the names of the other seven divisions. This may be done quite easily by referring to the various editions of the *Townland Index*, Lewis's *Topographical Dictionary of Ireland*, Ryan's *Irish Records: Sources for Family and Local History*, and *A New Genealogical Atlas of Ireland* (all of which have been dealt with in detail already).

For a number of reasons, this chart must be, at the initial stages at least, a provisional piece of work. Apart from the blank spaces in the names column, indicating where ancestors have not yet been identified, certain assumptions are made in filling in the chart which may prove to be incorrect. For the purposes of the chart it is assumed – in the absence of information to the contrary – that the family holding was the family home of the husband. There are two other possibilities. First, the holding could have been the childhood home of the wife, and her husband could have come 'cliamhain isteach', that is, married into the holding. Secondly, it's possible that the holding was newly taken and that neither the husband nor the wife had any previous history there.

Another factor to be considered is that the townland addresses of some members of the sixth generation are based on information under the heading 'Residence at the time of Marriage', in their children's marriage certificate. It is possible that the children were not living at home at the time of marriage and that the addresses given do not correspond to the home address.

The purpose of the second chart, Figure 9, is to help to establish which lines are likely to be most productive when more thoroughly researched. How to establish the information under the various heads has been dealt with already. The significance of most columns is self-evident. It is wiser to concentrate on an individual who lived in a parish in which Church records had an early commencement and for which the Religious Census of 1766 is extant, than on an individual who lived in an area without these advantages.

One of the greatest difficulties for the family historian is the problem of common surnames. The information from Matheson's *Special Report on Surnames in Ireland* and *Griffith's Valuation* should help the researcher to foresee the extent to which this difficulty is going to affect his research.

The population of a townland and the number of houses in it are significant for the researcher. These statistics are helpful both in the selection of lines for intensive research and in evaluating whatever information is collected.

Perhaps the most important, and certainly the most difficult fact to establish is whether or not estate records are available.

When both charts have been filled up with all available information, the selection of lines to be intensively researched is easy. Peig Murphy, number 19, is an obvious case for elimination: Murphy is a very common name in County Cork and there are twelve Murphy occupiers in the townland of Clonglaskan. On the other hand, John Nelan, number 27, seems an obvious choice for intensive research since the surname is one of the rarest in the entire chart and Kerry is not one of the counties in which it is principally found.

	NAME	COUNTY	BARONY	CIVIL PARISH	TOWNLAND
1 2	Benjamin Healy	Cork W.R.	Muskerry W	Clondrohid	Carriganimmy
3 4	Cors. Healy	Cork W.R	Muskerry W	Ballyvourney	Coolnacahera
5 6	Denis Riordan	Cork E.R.	Duhallow	Kilshannig	Gneeves
7 8	Timothy Kelleher Walsh	Cork E.R.	Muskerry E	Matehy	Dawstown
9 10	Johanna Dineen Denis Riordan	Cork W.R.	Muskerry W.	Kilnamartery	Renaniree
11 12	Catherine Riordan Patrick Lehane	Kerry	Magunihy	Killaha	Derryreag
13 14	Dineen	Kerry	Glanrought	Kilgarvan	Inchee
15 16	Mary Lehane Patk. O'Sullivan	Cork W.R.	Muskerry W.	Ballyvourney	Gortnascarty
17	Mary O'Sullivan	Cork W.K.	Bear	Kilcatherine	Bofikil
18	Darby O'Neill	Cork W.R.	Bear	Kilcatherine	Coulagh
19	Peig Murphy	Cork W.R.	Bear	Kilaconenagh	Clonglaskan
20	Jer O'Shea	Cork W.R.	Bear	Kilcatherine	Coulagh
21 22					
23 24	Margt. O'Sullivan Cors. Kelly	Cork W.R.	Bear	Kilcatherine	Caherkeen
25 26	Chas. McCarthy Ellen Dineen	Kerry	Clanmaurice	Kilcaragh	Liscullane
27	John Nelan	Kerry	Clanmaurice	Killury	Ballinglanna
28	Mary Murphy	Kerry	Clanmaurice	Killury	Farran
29 30	James Hickey	Cork W.R.	Carbery W.	Kilcrohane	Ballynatra
31 32					

Figure 8: Chart showing the sixth generation

CATHOLIC PARISH	POOR LAW UNION/SUPER REG. DIST.	PROBATE DISTRICT	CHURCH OF IRELAND DIOCESE
Clondrohid	Macroom	Cork	Cloyne
Ballyvourney	Macroom	Cork	Cloyne
Glountane	Mallow	Cork	Cloyne
Inniscarra	Cork	Cork	Cloyne
Kilnamartra	Macroom	Cork	Cloyne
Glenflesk	Killarney	Cork	Ardfert and Aghadoe
Kilgarvan	Killarney	Cork	Ardfert and Aghadoe
Ballyvourney	Macroom	Cork	Cloyne
Eyeries	Bantry	Cork	Ross
Eyeries	Bantry	Cork	Ross
Castletownbere	Bantry	Cork	Ross
Eyeries	Bantry	Cork	Ross
Eyeries	Bantry	Cork	Ross
Lixnaw	Listowel	Limerick	Artfert and Aghadoe
Causway	Listowel	Limerick	Artfert and Aghadoe
Causway	Listowel	Limereick	
Muintervara	Bantry	Cork	Cork

within eight important administrative divisions

	NAME	MATHESON NO. BIRTHS IRELAND	MATHESON MAINLY FOUND IN	NO. OCCUPIERS OF TOWNLAND BEARING SURNAME (GRIFFITH'S VAL)	POPULATION OF TOWNLAND 1841	1851	OCCUPIED HOUSES IN TOWNLAND NO. 1841	1851
1	Benjamin Healy	291	2/3 in Cork Kerry + 4	1	236	174	47	36
2			other Counties					
3	Cornelius Healy	291	As above	1	57	36	10	7
4								
5	Denis Riordan	159	89 in Cork	9	162	102	28	17
6								
7	Timothy Kelleher	148	92 in Cork	4	104	80	12	10
8	Walsh	932	large nos. everywhere					
9	Johanna Dineen	42	29 in Cork					
10	Denis Riordan	159	89 in Cork	1	65	5	11	11
11	Cath. Riordan	159	89 in Cork					
12	Patrick Lehane	30	29 in Cork	0				
13								
14	Dineen	42	29 in Cork	2	66	45	10	9
15	Mary Lehane	30	29 in Cork					
16	Patk. O'Sullivan	975	418 in Cork	1	51	36	10	6
17	Mary O'Sullivan	975	418 in Cork 50% in 4 Co's	2	179	85	35	16
18	Darby O'Neill	407	incl. Cork	6	143	252	26	44
19	Peig Murphy	1,386	About 500 in Cork	12	116	97	20	13
20	Jer O'Shea	46	Cork, Kerry Limerick	3	143	252	26	44
21								
22								
23	Margt.O'Sullivan	975	418 in Cork All over Irl.					
24	Cors. Kelly	1,242	Large nos. in Cork.	4	193	263	36	48
25	Chas. McCarthy	498	Common in Kerry	4	81	64	12	10
26	Ellen Dineen	42	29 in Cork					
27	John Nelan	49	Clare, Gal. Rosc. Sligo. About	2	196	144	26	20
28	Mary Murphy	1,386	500 in Cork	1	158	68	24	12
29	James Hickey	139	Common in 5 Co's Incl. Cork	1	45	26	7	4
30								
31								
32								

Figure 9: Information chart to facilitate

ESTATE RECORDS		LOCATED	PARISH REGISTER YEAR BEGUN	RELIGIOUS CENSUS EXTANT	HEARTH MONEY ROLLS EXTANT
LANDLORD'S NAME	AREA HELD				
Massy. H Massy	13,363		1807	Yes	No
Henry Leader	9 Leader landowners in Cork		1825	Yes	No
Silver C. Oliver	9,872	Yes	1829	Yes	No
Chas. Putland	5,300	Yes	1814	Yes	No
Herbt. Baldwin	4 Baldwin landowners in Cork.		1803	Yes	No
James B. Hewson	5 Hewson landowners in Kerry		1818	No	No
Sir. Geo. Colthurst	31,260	Yes	1825	No	No
Earl of Bantry	69,500	Yes	1824	No	No
Earl of Bantry	69,500	Yes	1824	No	No
John L. Puxley	9,158	No	1819	No	No
Earl of Bantry	69,500	Yes	1824	No	No
John L. Puxley	9,158	No	1824	No	No
Earl of Listowel	31,505	Yes	1810	No	No
Timothy O'Connor	778	No	1782	No	No
Timothy O'Connor	778	No	1782	No	No
J. B. Gumbleton	884	No	1819	No	No

the selection of lines for further research

With the guidance of the charts, modified by a bias towards as wide a geographical spread as possible, I selected five lines for thorough investigation: 5, Denis Riordan; 7, Timothy Kelleher; 16, Patrick Sullivan; 25, Charles McCarthy; 27, John Nelan.

STAGE IV

Research on John Nelan, number 27, did not proceed very far. The records of the parish of Killury and Ratoo (Causeway) were in bad handwriting and on faded paper. Some parts were illegible. The amount of time required to make progress seemed excessive.

Patrick Sullivan's farm, according to the tithe applotment book for the parish of Ballyvourney, was occupied by Michael Leehane in 1827. Since Patrick Sullivan's wife was Mary Lehane it seems reasonable to assume that Michael was her father and that her husband married into the farm. The only full rentals in the Colthurst estate papers were dated 1886-95 – too late to be helpful. An earlier rental, dated 1839, appeared to be a list of leaseholders. Only 46 names were listed in this document, whereas there were over 200 in the later rentals. Neither Sullivan nor Lehane, nor indeed the townland of Gortnascarty, was referred to in the 1839 document. Further progress here was not possible.

RIORDAN FAMILY

The documents that were examined and the problems that arose in researching Denis Riordan and Timothy Kelleher were so alike it would be repetitious to deal with both, so I will deal with Denis Riordan only.

Denis Riordan's son Timothy, and some of his grandchildren, were buried in an old family grave in Abbey's Well Cemetery (also known as Kilgobnait). The grave, eight plots wide, has a stone with an inscription which is still legible: 'Here lies the body of Edmd Riordan who died July 21 1767 aged 75 years, his wife and family's burying place.'

This was one of the principal attractions of researching the Riordan line. My objective was to try to trace a connection between Denis Riordan and Edmund Riordan, who, according to the gravestone, would have been born in 1692. I was aware from the start that the grave was a typical 'communal grave', and that the likelihood of Edmund Riordan of the gravestone being in the direct line of the Riordans whom I was tracing was rather remote. The existence of the Religious Census of 1766 for the parish of Kilshannig was an added inducement, however. On the other hand, *Griffith's Valuation*, which indicated that there were nine Riordan occupiers in the townland of Gneeves, gave me little ground for optimism.

None of the nine Riordans listed under the townland of Gneeves in *Griffith's Valuation* was called Denis. My first task was to try to connect Denis with one of the nine. The 'cancelled books' indicated that Timothy, Denis's son, had taken over the farm from Margaret Riordan in 1866. One of the nine Riordans in *Griffith's Valuation* was called Margaret.

I then examined the tenure book and the house book for the parish of Kilshannig. (There was no field book.) They were dated 27 July 1848. The house book had been extensively revised. The dates of the revisions – unlike those of the 'cancelled books' – were not shown. In 1848 there were 11 Riordans holding land in Gneeves. A further complication was that the lot numbers used in the various record books did not correspond. It seemed that consolidation of holdings was in full swing and lot numbers were being constantly updated to reflect a changing situation. Despite these difficulties, certain facts could be established. According to the tenure book, Denis Riordan's land was in several parcels. He had taken 31-year leases on two farms, one in 1828 and the other in 1830. The tenure book also stated that Denis Riordan 'lives in lot 8'. Around 1850, revisions of the house book record some significant changes. Denis Riordan's holdings are split in half. Margaret Riordan is proprietor of one half, including lot 8, and Denis Riordan is in possession of the rest; he now lives in a different house.

Adding the valuation data to information already gathered from old people, it appears that the original Denis Riordan died around 1850; that his widow, Margaret, continued to live on in the family house and to work the smaller of the farms, while one of his sons, also Denis, took possession of the larger farm and the house that went with it. It seems clear then that Denis and Margaret Riordan had at least two sons, Denis and Timmy.

The valuation records suggested the existence of relationships between some of the 11 Riordan occupiers. The most interesting source for speculation was the fact that Denis Riordan senior held some mountain land in common with Patrick Riordan. Also, Patrick and Denis senior each held farms under identical conditions: both farms were leased in 1830 for 31 years at £16.10s.0d. per year. This suggests that Patrick and Denis senior were brothers who had each inherited half of a larger farm; or that Patrick was an older son of Denis senior, who had been given his portion before his father's death. However, without more evidence, no firm conclusions could be drawn.

I turned my attention next to the tithe applotment book for the civil parish of Kilshannig, dated 25 July 1836. This book indicated that five Riordans held land in the townland of Gneeves. One was named Denis. There was no Patrick. This inclined me towards the belief that Patrick was Denis senior's son rather than his brother.

I continued my study of the Riordan family by examining the baptismal records of the parish of Glountane. They were not of good quality. For most entries, the townland in which the child was born is not given. The section of the register that deals with the period April 1842 to August 1844 was almost illegible. Much of the rest of it was quite difficult to decipher. I found seven of the children of Denis Riordan junior and seven of those of Timmy Riordan and Ellen Kelleher. However, it was the earlier generations that I was most interested in finding.

The parish records begin in the year 1829 and this is likely to be too late to include the baptismal entries of Denis junior and Timmy. I located a baptismal entry in 1831 of a James Riordan whose father was Denis Riordan and whose mother was Margaret Brien; no townland was given. This could be a younger brother of Denis junior and Timmy.

I drew up a Riordan family tree diagram based on fact and speculation. The bold lines represent reasonable certainty; the faint lines represent guesswork supported by interpretation of records.

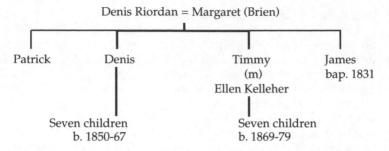

Denis Riordan = Margaret (Brien)

Patrick   Denis   Timmy   James
(m)   bap. 1831
Ellen Kelleher

Seven children   Seven children
b. 1850-67   b. 1869-79

At this point I was still about two generations away from the gravestone inscription and the Religious Census, both with dates in the 1760s. Three sets of records remained to be examined: the records in the Registry of Deeds; estate records; wills. First of all I eliminated the Registry of Deeds as a likely source. Though the tenure book showed that the Riordans had leases, they held them from the Oliver family, who owned almost 10,000 acres. The leases would not have been registered in the Registry of Deeds but kept with the estate papers. No relevant Riordan wills appear in W. P. W. Phillimore's *Index to Irish Wills*, vol. II. That left only the estate papers.

I found the name of the Riordan landlord, Silver C. Oliver, in *Griffith's Valuation*. The only Oliver referred to in Hayes's *Manuscript Sources for the History of Irish Civilization* was in the following entry: 'Oliver (family of) Ainsworth (J. F.) report on the Oliver papers (from 1584), now in the National Library of Ireland, relating to the Oliver and Silver families of Castle Oliver, Co. Limerick and to properties in Cos. Limerick, Leitrim, Kerry, Cork, Kilkenny, Waterford . . . (Nat. Lib. rep. on private collections, no. 395).'

All these reports are available for consultation at the Genealogical Office, Kildare Street, Dublin. There were 11 foolscap-size pages of typescript in report number 395. It was bound in a volume with over 40 similar reports on other sets of estate papers. The report on the Oliver papers was divided into 11 sections, with headings like 'Testamentary', 'Co. Kerry Estates', 'Co. Cork Estates'. In the section on County Cork estates there was no reference to the barony of Duhallow or to tenants. Most of the material in the collection was on the Limerick estates. I had drawn a blank with estate papers.

I decided to examine the 1766 census, more out of interest now than with any hope of being able to connect up the Riordans listed in it. A copy of the Religious Census for the whole diocese of Cloyne is available in the National Archives. It was 'carefully and accurately transcribed from the original records and returns kept in the Public Record Office, by the Rev. Barth^w O'Keeffe D.D. Priest of the Diocese of Cloyne, 1904'.

The census lists a total of 409 Catholic and 61 Protestant families in the parish of Kilshannig. The families are listed under 19 'districts', and nine Riordan families appear spread over seven districts. There was an Edmund Riordan listed in the Gortroe district, very possibly the Edmund of the gravestone inscription, since the Religious Census was taken no later than April 1766, more than a year before his death.

There was no reference to Gneeves in the part of the census dealing with Kilshannig. The modern civil parish of Kilshannig has 63 townlands. Allowing for the divisions of townlands made by the Ordnance Survey, it still has a total of 53 townlands compared to the 19 'districts' listed in the Religious Census. The names of 17 of the districts correspond with the names of 17 modern townlands. Interesting as this was, I did not delve further into the matter as it was not going to advance my knowledge of the Riordan family.

At this point I had exhausted all sources of information about the Riordan family. I was left with many loose ends and I had failed to achieve my main objective. A far more thorough knowledge of later generations was some consolation for not being able to identify the earlier ones.

McCARTHY FAMILY

A grand-aunt who lived to be 92 gave me very detailed information about the McCarthys of Liscullane, Lixnaw, County Kerry. During her childhood three McCarthy families lived on adjacent farms in the townland of Liscullane. Two of the proprietors, William, known as 'Liam Rua', and Patrick, were related. Her own father, William Charles, was related, but not as closely, to these two families. There was a fourth McCarthy family, that of Peter McCarthy, in a different part of the townland, which was tenuously linked to the other three. She was unable to be more specific as to the degrees of relationship.

The first step I took was to locate the baptismal entry of Charles McCarthy and those of his only brother and sister:

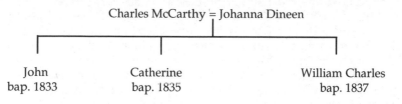

With the benefit of exact dates to guide me, I continued with my search of the Lixnaw parish records, this time trying to find the baptismal entry of Charles McCarthy, the father of the above family. The records, which started in 1810, were very good. They gave the townland address of families that were the subject of entries. I located six children who were born in Liscullane to the same McCarthy parents:

William McCarthy = Mary Connell

John	Peter	William	Charles	Honora	Catherine
1811	1813	1815	1817	1821	1823

At first I thought I had added another generation to the family tree and connected up all the McCarthy families of Liscullane. On closer examination, however, it appeared unlikely that the Charles I had found was the Charles I was looking for. My Charles was born in 1817. He would have to have married at 15 years of age to have fathered John in 1833. This seemed improbable.

To get some idea of Charles McCarthy's date of birth I attempted to locate his death register entry, where his age at death would be given. I did not know when he died so I examined the cancelled books for Liscullane. I found that Charles

McCarthy's name was crossed out and replaced by that of his son in 1873. I wrote to the Superintendent Registrar's Office in Killarney requesting a copy of the death entry of Charles McCarthy of Liscullane who died during or after the year 1873. I received the information three weeks later: Charles McCarthy died in 1879 aged 81 years, which meant that he was born in 1798. Even though ages in death registers are not very reliable, this reinforced the suspicion that the Charles McCarthy born in 1817 was not the one I was looking for. It appeared that I had constructed the family tree of one of the other Liscullane families. As all of the families were closely related it was not surprising that the same Christian names cropped up.

I decided to approach the matter from a different angle. Since all the families were related, it followed that they must have shared common ancestors some generations back. By tracing all the McCarthy lines, I felt that I would be taking advantage of all available clues and thereby would be more likely to achieve my objective of discovering earlier generations.

I returned to the cancelled books to trace back William Charles, Patrick and Liam Rua (William). I already knew that William Charles's father was Charles. My grand-aunt had told me that Patrick's father was 'Billin' – William again. The cancelled books indicated that William Charles got his holding from Charles, as already stated, and that Liam Rua got his from John. The chain of possession was longer in the case of Patrick. It worked out as follows: Patrick – Mary – William (Billin) – Mary.

I interpreted this as meaning that Patrick got his holding from his mother, Mary, who in turn got it from her husband, William (Billin), whom she outlived. A baptismal entry dated March 1855 lent weight to this interpretation. It concerned the baptism of Patrick, son of William McCarthy and Mary Fitzmaurice of Liscullane. The Mary from whom Billin got the holding I assumed to be his mother.

A very valuable feature of the cancelled books, and indeed of all valuation records, is that when two or more landholders in a townland have identical names, to distinguish them from one another the Christian names of their respective fathers are bracketed after their names. Thus, to distinguish the two

Williams, Liam Rua and Billin, that were landholders in Liscullane in the 1870s, they are listed thus: 'William McCarthy (John)'; 'William McCarthy(Wm)'.

I already knew that William's (Liam Rua's) father was John. The form of William used for Patrick's father – 'Billin' or 'Little William' – suggested that his father's name was William. The cancelled books confirmed this. Clearly, Billin was none other than William who was born to William McCarthy and Mary Connell in 1815.

I went on to examine *Griffith's Valuation* for Liscullane townland. Five McCarthys were listed; Charles, Mary and John, all of whom I have already dealt with; James (whose name was crossed out in 1861 and whose holding was absorbed by Charles); and Peter. I was able to procure from the Valuation Office a copy of the map to which *Griffith's Valuation* is keyed. Houses, farm buildings and farm boundaries were marked on the map and easily identifiable. Numbers and letters on the map are keyed to the numbers and letters in the column in *Griffith's Valuation* headed 'no. and letters of reference to map'. Apart from Peter, who had a separate 60-acre farm, the McCarthys appeared to be sharing a 190-acre tract of land. There was no indication of separate plots for each of the four families. The four houses were close together and in the centre of the large holding.

The tenure book, dated July 1849, listed five McCarthys as occupiers of the 190-acre holding. It also gave the proportion held by each: 'Charles McCarthy $^1/_5$th; James McCarthy $^2/_{15}$ths; Mary McCarthy $^1/_6$th; John McCarthy (Wm.) $^1/_6$th; John McCarthy (Peter) $^1/_3$rd.'

The following information was on the same page: 'Lease 1839 for 21 years, rent in lease £130 per year, in common.' It appeared from the proportions held by each that the holding had been divided into thirds and that some of the thirds had undergone further subdivision. The fact that there were two John McCarthys listed meant that their fathers' names were bracketed after their own names. Thus, there was a John McCarthy whose father was Peter and a John McCarthy whose father was William.

It seemed likely that John McCarthy (William) was the John

born in 1811 to William McCarthy and Mary Connell. This would make Liam Rua and Patrick – whom my grand-aunt believed to be closely related – first cousins. The portion held by John, which was half of his father's share, makes this interpretation even more likely.

The house book, dated July 1849, listed the same McCarthys. This book was revised in May 1851, at which point John McCarthy (Peter) was crossed off, possibly indicating that he was an old man who died at this stage.

I examined the tithe applotment book for the parish of Kilcaragh, but the only information given concerning the occupiers of Liscullane was 'McCarthys and Moloney', followed by the amount payable in 'tythes'.

I was more fortunate with the estate records. The landlord, whose name I got from *Griffith's Valuation*, was the Earl of Listowel. *Burke's Baronetage and Peerage* identified him as William Hare, Second Earl of Listowel. In his book *Discovering Kerry*, T. J. Barrington gives a little background information to the Hare holdings in Kerry: 'There is a title, Earl of Listowel, borne by the Hare family. A Cork businessman of English descent, Richard bought in 1783 the Listowel properties of the Earl of Kerry . . .'

Hayes's *Manuscript Sources for the History of Irish Civilization* refers to a collection of estate papers in the National Archives 'relating to the estates in the Cos. Cork and Kerry of the (Hare family) Earls of Listowel 18th C.', and to a second collection in the Public Record Office of Northern Ireland.

The Dublin collection was disappointing. I examined the items which, from the description in the manuscript catalogue, seemed to be the most relevant: M2348: 'Descriptive notes on some Kerry farms, probably on the Earl of Listowel's Estates, 1790'. This little notebook, stitched together with hairy twine, was interesting. It described various farms and tenures but there was no reference to McCarthys or Liscullane. M2353: 'Copy of Lord Kerry's rent roll for Lixnaw and lands in neighbourhood N.D., 1780s.' The rent roll was tattered and difficult to read. It was dated around 1750. I failed again to find either McCarthys or Liscullane.

I wrote to the Public Record Office of Northern Ireland for a detailed list of the items in their Earl of Listowel papers, and then ordered photocopies of the most pertinent papers. The two most interesting items I received were 'Memorials' – formal statements of fact followed by petitions.

The earlier of the two memorials was dated 22 March 1842. It was from John, Charles, Peter and Mary (widow) McCarthy and William Behane, all of Liscullane, to the Earl of Listowel. It was written

in the hope your Lordship in your usual humanity will alleviate the burden we labour under, that is to say, the enormous rent we are charged with for our lands. Permit us, my Lord, to inform you that we John, Charles and the widow McCarthy are joint tenants . . . and since the death of Mr Garham, whose life the Yielding family had of the lands, have improved same at great expense, by draining, ditching . . . Permit us also my Lord to inform you that we, Peter McCarthy and Wm. Behane, of the woodland division of Liscullane adjoining the river Brick, have laid out each £80 in draining, ditching and improving our farms . . . We implore your Lordship's benevolent notice of this our appeal to take into your noble consideration, our present situation, paying more rent now, than the middleman Yielding taxed us with . . .

Another document in the Belfast collection, entitled 'Particulars of the proposals made for the Right Honourable the Earl of Listowel's estate in the County of Kerry', gave a good insight into the background to this appeal for a rent reduction. It appears that when an old lease expired, the resident tenants did not have their tenures automatically renewed. Tenders were solicited from the public at large and the holding was given to whoever happened to make the best offer. The 1829 document lists the applicants for farms that were to be relet, the offers made by the applicants, and the opinion of the land agent on each applicant. The document seems to have been prepared to enable the Earl of Listowel to select those to whom he would let farms. Some of the land agent's comments are very revealing:

John Hourigan: The occupying tenant – his family have resided here I understand for 50 years. From a comparison with other proposals he does not appear to have offered the value . . . John Buckley: Is solvent and of good character but has I conceive offered more than the lands are worth.'

Out of 40 applicants, the agent thought that 11 had offered

more than the land was worth. He considered that the proposals of four occupying tenants were too low.

According to the tenure book, the McCarthys took a lease on their holding in 1839. This must have been a renewal of an earlier lease or rental agreement as the tithe applotment book and Church records indicated that they were in the townland since at least 1811. It would appear that when their holding was put on the market in 1839, they were forced to offer an excessive rent in order to retain possession.

It seems that imposing excessive rents and granting reductions in lieu of improvements was widespread. The following comment in the same document shows the land agent's thoughts on the matter: 'James Connor: A man of very good character and solvent . . . he has offered more than I think the lands are worth but by allowing him for the first four or five years £10 or £12 a year for the improvement of the land.'

When I examined the Putland estate papers in relation to the Kelleher family of Dawstown, Blarney, I found references to the same procedure: '1817 April: Allowance Darby Kelleher for a stable and cowhouse built at Dawstown £34.' James S. Donnelly, Jr deals with the practice in detail in *The Land and the People in Nineteenth Century Cork*.

The tenure book gives the impression that the McCarthys' appeal was successful. It states that the rent in the lease of 1839 was £130, but the rent being paid in 1849 was £95.

The second memorial is from Peter McCarthy of 'Lisgillane' to the Earl of Listowel, dated November 1842. It relates a tale of misfortune and requests unspecified help. Peter McCarthy, while doing reconstruction work on his house, used his large barn to store his furniture and temporarily to house his five children and three servants. The barn burned to the ground destroying all his furniture: 'Were it not for Devine Providence and the assistance of his neighbours, memoralist's children would have become victims of the flames.'

The first paragraph was the most interesting, in which Peter McCarthy identified himself to the Earl of Listowel: 'The humble memorial of Peter McCarthy of Lisgillane, part of your Lordship's Estate in Kerry – Most respectfully sheweth – that memoralist is the son of John McCarthy who is a resident tenant on said lands, and your Lordship's memoralist, the third generation residing thereon.'

The information in the memorials enabled me to tidy up some loose ends. It is clear from both memorials that Peter McCarthy was living on the separate 60-acre farm. He was not the Peter born to William McCarthy and Mary Connell in 1813 – he gives his father's name as John. This had to be John McCarthy (Peter) rather than John McCarthy (William), because Peter was married with five children in 1842 and it is not possible that his father could have been born as late as 1811. Peter states that he was the third generation of McCarthys to occupy Liscullane, which meant his grandfather, Peter McCarthy, was the first or one of the first McCarthys to come to Liscullane.

I drew a family tree of the McCarthys of Liscullane based on the most reasonable interpretation of the facts (Figure 10). The earliest generation is made up of Peter and John, whom I would suspect to be brothers. John does not appear in any of the records. I am basing his existence on two pieces of evidence: my grand-aunt's assurance that the families that descended from William and Charles were related, and the fact that the eldest sons of both William and Charles were named John. This is in line with the very strong tradition of calling the eldest son after his paternal grandfather.

I discovered by reading through their indexes that the Cork Archives has a collection of the Earl of Listowel's estate papers. Most of the material concerned lands in Cork, but I unearthed one very interesting item: 'Copy Deed of Conveyance dated 28 day of Feb. 1783, The Rt. Hon. Francis Thomas Earl of Kerry to Richard Hare Esq.'

Listed at the back of the conveyance were all the then current leases on the land being sold. Liscullane, according to this document, was leased to Theophilius Yielding from 23 March 1776 for three lives, namely those of Theophilius Yielding, Richard Crosbie Sandes and James Garham. This explained the references in the memorial of March 1842 to 'the middleman Yielding' and the death of Mr Gorham. Mr Gorham (or Garham) was clearly the last of the 'three lives' to survive, and on his death, Liscullane reverted to the Earl of Listowel, who let

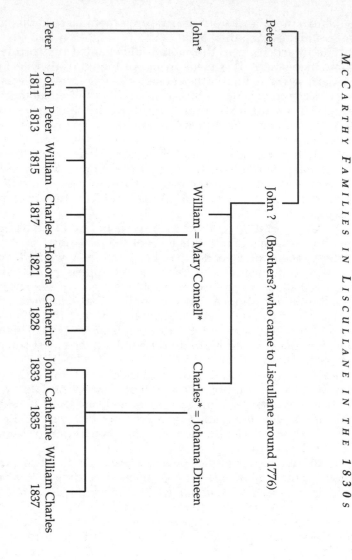

Figure 10: Family tree of McCarthys
of Liscullane

it directly to the tenants. It was also clear that there would be no reference to the McCarthys of Liscullane in the Earl of Listowel's estate papers before 1839. Up to that date the immediate landlord was Theophilius Yielding and his heirs. I failed to find any Yielding papers but it is reasonable to assume that Peter and John McCarthy came to Liscullane in 1776 as tenants of Theophilius Yielding.

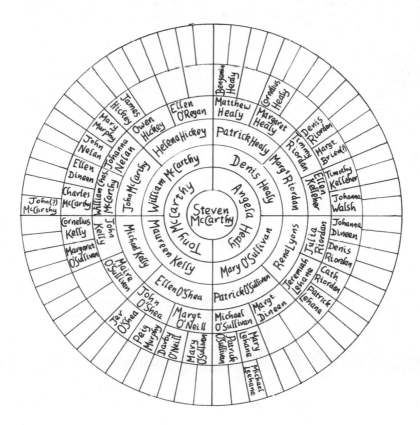

Figure 11: Family circle chart with names added at Stage IV

Neither the Religious Census of 1766 nor hearth money rolls survive for the parish of Kilcaragh; nor was I able to find relevant wills or gravestone inscriptions. A search in the Registry of Deeds for Yielding/McCarthy leases proved fruitless. No more information was available on the McCarthys of Liscullane.

Figure 10 illustrates the relationships between the various McCarthy families resident in Liscullane in the 1830s. It is based on an interpretation of all the information I could gather from the various archives.

Figure 11 shows to what extent I was able to fill in my family circle chart after completing the four stages of research.

DEGREE OF SUCCESS TO BE EXPECTED

The time and effort spent in trying to extend the family circle beyond the sixth generation on the chart was disappointingly unproductive. I was unable to trace the lines I researched intensively beyond the period 1775 to 1825. It is not reasonable to draw conclusions from such a small sample. However, the few published pedigrees from the same social group that I was able to locate are consistent with my own findings.

President John F. Kennedy was probably the most distinguished man to have descended from Irish Catholic tenant farmer stock. On St Patrick's Day 1961 the Irish Ambassador to Washington presented to President Kennedy a grant of a Coat of Arms and a genealogical chart showing the President's immediate descent and the background of the Kennedys in Ireland. The documents were prepared by the Chief Herald at the Genealogical Office, Dublin. I was unable to locate any published version of the chart, though the Coat of Arms was published in *The Irish Times* on 18 March 1961. On application to the Genealogical Office I received a genealogical chart of the Kennedys of Dunganstown, Co. Wexford. The earliest direct Kennedy ancestor that could be traced was the president's great-grandfather, Patrick Kennedy, who was born about 1823.

Ronald Reagan was another descendant of the Irish Catholic tenantry who reached the highest office in the USA. Debrett's traced his Irish roots. The earliest record they located was the baptismal entry of his great-grandfather Michael O'Regan, dated 3 September 1829. However, from the information in that entry they got the names of the parents of Michael O'Regan and so, in a sense, extended the Regan line into the previous century.

Perhaps because both pedigrees were disappointingly short, attempts were made to lengthen them, and, by means of a

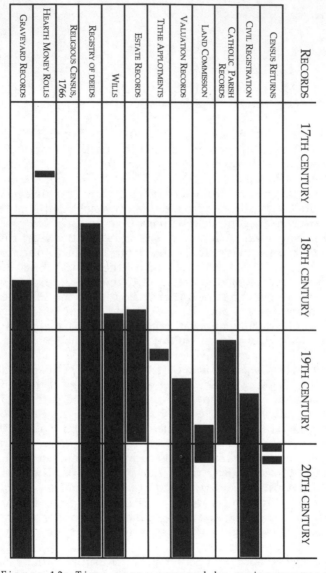

Figure 12: Time-spans covered by major sources

series of imaginative leaps, both presidents were connected to Brian Boru. Kennedy and Reagan, it would appear, are descended from Cinnéidigh and Riagán respectively, both nephews of Brian Boru. This is reminiscent of the pedigrees which traced descent from Adam or even from the gods, and is to be taken as seriously.

The documented pedigrees of Kennedy and Reagan come to an end at the beginning of the nineteenth century. The resources, prestige and professional skill of the Genealogical Office and Debrett's are such that we can confidently assume that all relevant documents were examined and nothing remains to be discovered. General conclusions cannot be drawn from two examples, though they give some indication of what to expect.

In the absence of a large and accessible collection of conscientiously researched pedigrees of tenant farmer stock, our expectations of success must be guided for the most part by the actual or estimated starting dates of relevant records. The time-span covered by each of the twelve major sources is represented in Figure 12. It should be remembered when interpreting this chart that a marriage recorded in 1820 is likely to have been contracted between parties that were born in the previous century. A person whose death was registered in the 1860s could, taking an extreme example, have been born in the 1770s. This chart offers a rough guide as to how optimistic you can reasonably expect to be.

6

STORAGE AND RETRIEVAL

I have found it entirely satisfactory to allow the nature of the material to determine how it is stored, and to use the family circle chart, which I have already referred to several times, as the basis of a system of indexation.

Living testimony, transcriptions, abstractions, accounts of searches, and other suitable material, are all written on A4 pages, numbered from one upwards as they come to hand, and stored in loose-leaf binders. Bulkier items such as books and letters are stored in files, which, like the pages, are numbered. These binders and files constitute your research notes.

A special loose-leaf binder is used as an index. On the first page of this index is the family circle chart, with the names of ancestors supplied insofar as they are known – as more names are identified they are written into the appropriate segments. Each ancestor is given a number which is written into his/her section. You can start, for example, at the twelve o'clock position with your grandparents and number them clockwise, 1, 2, 3 and 4; then move into the segment for great-grand-parents and number them 5 to 12, and so on. Figure 13 is a reproduction of the family circle chart which I constructed of my own family at an early stage of research.

A separate page of this loose-leaf binder index is then al-lotted to each ancestor. It should be clear that this index is something that grows with the notes. It enlarges as more an-cestors are identified.

If this system is to work, every new item added to the notes must be indexed. For example, when I transcribed the infor-mation relating to Patrick Healy from the Superintendent Registrar's Office, Cork (Figure 14), I already had 37 pages of notes. Thus, this became page 38.

To index page 38 of the notes, I had to turn to the appropri-ate pages of the index: page 5 for Patrick, page 13 for Matthew

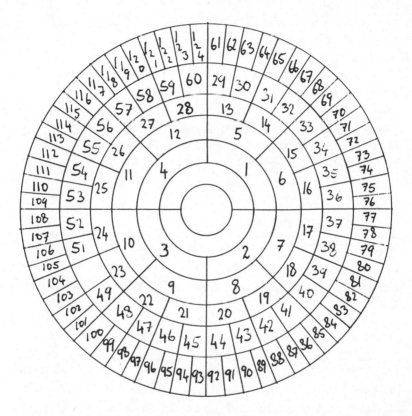

Figure 13: Family circle chart at an early stage of
research, numbered for use as an index

38
Notes.

14 August 1980.

Superintendent Registrar's Office, Liberty St., Cork.

I examined the birth registers of the Slieveragh District, Macroom, for the birth entry of Patrick Healy. I located a likely entry and then I searched for brothers and sisters. I located only one, a brother, Daniel. I searched registers covering the period 1: January: 1864 to 4: December: 1893. Both entries are transcribed below.

Date and Place of Birth	Name	Sex	Name and Surname and dwelling of Father.	Name and Surname and maiden name of Mother	Rank or Profession of Father	Signature Qualification and Residence of Informant
17: March: 1871 Ballymakira Ballyvourney	Patrick	M	Matthew Healy Ballymakira	Margaret Healy formerly Healy	Publican	Matthew Healy Father Ballymakira
20: April: 1869 Ballymakira Ballyvourney	Daniel	M	Matthew Healy Ballymakira	Margaret Healy formerly Healy	Publican.	Matthew Healy Father Ballymakira.

Figure 14: Page 38 of notes

5
Index

Patrick Healy

Notes:

page 36 : Extracts from 1901 Census Return.

page 38 : Birth Register entries of Patrick and Daniel Healy.

page 43 : Healys - Death Register search.

page 47 : Family tree chart.

page 56 : Death notices and graveyard record extracts.

page 73 : Marriage Register entry of Denis Healy.

page 90 : Reply to enquiry to U.S.A. re. death of Daniel Healy.

page 117 : Letter from Cork Distillery re Patrick Healy's employment there as a farrier.

page 154 : Letter to P.P., Ballyvourney enquiring about dates of Parish Records.

Files:

File no 1. : Ballyvourney Parish - Gravestone Inscriptions - photocopy.

File no 4 : Patrick Healy's Baptismal; marriage (church); marriage (state); and death certificates.

Figure 15: Page 5 of index

and page 14 for Margaret. On each of those pages I wrote: 'Birth Register entries of Patrick and Daniel Healy; Notes, page 38.'

Retrieving information is quite simple. Find the name of the ancestor in whom you are interested in the family circle of the index. The number corresponding to his or her name will lead to his or her special page of the index. Written after the name on that page should be the numbers of the pages in the notes and the numbers of the files where information on this individual may be found, provided, of course, that indexing has been conscientiously carried out. Figure 15 is a facsimile of page 5 of my index, i.e. the page relating to Patrick Healy.

This may seem to be a tedious and time-consuming activity, but when you consider the number of individuals being re-searched and the fact that family history may become a life-time hobby, dropped for long periods, it becomes clear that it is essential to use a foolproof method of retrieving the in-formation collected about each individua, easily and quickly. This system of indexation makes it possible for several people to participate in researching a family, and for someone else to take up the work after the instigator has himself become food for genealogists.

7

FUTURE OF IRISH GENEALOGY

There have been very significant developments in Irish genealogy during the past ten years and it is envisaged that by the end of the millenium, there will be even greater growth and resources available.

High unemployment in Ireland has been good for genealogy. In the early 1980s, in order to give work experience to unemployed young people, AnCo began to work in conjunction with various groups involved in the indexing of parish registers. In Offaly twenty young people were employed on a training scheme in 1983 which had the objective of preparing indexes to the parish registers of all parishes and all religious denominations within Offaly up to the year 1900. Similar parish register indexing schemes were set up in Clare, Tipperary, Limerick, Monaghan, Carlow, Longford, Westmeath, Wicklow and Waterford. These projects were all locally based and the question of standards was left to the individual organizations.

In many of these areas, local genealogical centres grew out of this work. The advantages of having some kind of central organization was obvious and representatives of various genealogical centres came together and formed an umbrella organization called the Irish Family History Co-operative, or the IFHC for short.

In 1988 the IFHC teamed up with other groups which, for one reason or another, have an interest in Irish genealogy; Bord Fáilte and a committee from the Taoiseach's office being the most important. The National Genealogical Project grew out of this combination of interests.

The National Genealogical Project aims to computerize all genealogical material and to provide a network of family research centres throughout the entire country. People interested in their roots will be directed by a central body to the centre or centres where the records relevant to their researches are to be found. It is planned to have one research centre per county, though some of the more populous counties may have two.

This ambitious project is far from completion. There are very many problems to be solved, which range from technical problems concerning computers to legal problems associated with copyright. Some local centres are well advanced and functioning, while others are barely started.

The Corofin Centre, catering for County Clare, is the type of operation on which local centres are likely to model themselves. It has been fully operational for a number of years as a non-profit-making body run by the local development association. It needs to be self-financing, however, so there is a charge for its services – £40 for a preliminary search and further charges for a more detailed investigation, up to a ceiling of £100. The centre deals with both postal and personal enquiries. Those interested in using its services are asked to fill up a standard search form. The staff then carry out a genealogical search using the centre's wide range of sources. These include: indexed parish registers, both Catholic and Church of Ireland – it appears that there are no Presbyterian records for the county, gravestone inscriptions, 1901 census returns (microfilm), shipping records, school rolls, and newspapers. While the state registers of births, deaths and marriages are not on the premises, the centre has access to them.

The centre receives about a thousand enquiries each year, though not all of them are followed through. Most visitors who want their roots traced prefer to let the staff of the centre do the work and to get on with their holiday themselves. About one in ten shows an interest in personal involvement in the research. To facilitate those, the Corofin Centre is in the process of building an extension with library and research facilities which will be open to the public.

Unfortunately, the Corofin Centre is the exception and not the rule. At present, partial service or no service at all is the norm in most counties. However, even a partial service could be very useful. Such a service usually means that some of the parish registers for the county have been indexed and that the centre, though not really open for business, will attempt to answer specific, but not general, enquiries.

Recently, interests in the North of Ireland have become associated with the project, which is now known as the Irish Genealogical Project. The International Fund for Ireland has provided $1.5 million towards the costs of the project and £1 million is forthcoming from the EC structural fund. It is clear that the situation is constantly changing. The Genealogical Office or the Irish Family History Foundation (1 Clarinda Park North, Dún Laoghaire, Dublin) should be able to give an update on the addresses of the various centres throughout the country and the services that they provide.

BIBLIOGRAPHY AND SOURCES

A Collection of the Public Statutes passed in the First and Second Year of the Reign of her Majesty Queen Victoria (George and John Grierson; Dublin 1838).

Barrington, T. J., *Discovering Kerry* (Blackwater: Dublin 1976).

Beckett, J. C., *The Making of Modern Ireland* (Faber and Faber: London 1966).

Begley, D. F. (ed.), *Irish Genealogy: A Record Finder* (Heraldic Artists Ltd: Dublin 1981).

Bord Fáilte, *Clan Rallies in Ireland, 1990* (Information Sheet No. 41); *Tracing Your Ancestors* (Information Sheet No. 021).

Breffney, B. de, Review of the *Genealogist's Encyclopaedia* in *The Irish Ancestor*, vol. l, no. 2, 1969-70, p. 146.

Brooke-Little, J. (ed.), *Boutell's Heraldry* (Frederick Warne: London and N.Y. 1978).

British Parliamentary Papers, 1851, Census Ireland Population 12 (Irish University Press: Shannon 1968).

British Parliamentary Papers: Copy of a return of the names of proprietors and the area and valuation of all properties in the several counties of Ireland, held in fee or perpetuity, or on long leases at chief , prepared for the use of her majesty's government and printed by Alexander Thom 87 and 88, Abbey Street, Dublin, by the direction of the Irish Government and at the expense of the treasury, House of Commons, 1876.

Burke's Genealogical and Heraldic History of the Peerage, Baronetage and Knightage, P. Townsend (ed.) (Burke's Peerage Ltd: London 1967).

Burke's Irish Family Records (Burke's Peerage Ltd: London 1976).

Burke, H., *The People and the Poor Law in 19th Century Ireland* (WEB: West Sussex 1987).

Byrne, Michael, 'Irish Parish Register Indexing Projects' in *Journal of the Irish Family History Society*, vol. I, 1985.

Camp, A. J., *Tracing Your Ancestry* (John Gifford Ltd: 1970).

Casey, A. E. (ed.), *O'Kief Coshe Mang, Slieve Lougher and Upper*

Blackwater in Ireland (Privately 1966).

Clare, Rev. W., *A Simple Guide to Irish Genealogy* (Geo. E. J. Coldwell Ltd: London 1938).

Collins, M. E., *An Outline of Modern Irish History* (The Educational Company: 1974)

Connell, K. H., *The Population of Ireland, 1750-1845* (Oxford: Clarendon Press 1950).

Debrett's Guide to Tracing your Ancestors (Webb and Bower Ltd: Exeter 1981).

Falley, M. D., *Irish and Scotch-Irish Ancestral Research* (Shenandoah Publishing House: Virginia 1962).

Donnelly, J. S., *The Land and the People of Nineteenth Century Cork* (Routledge & Kegan Paul: London & Boston 1975).

Edwards, R. D., *A New History of Ireland* (Gill and Macmillan: Dublin 1972).

Eustace, P. B. (ed.), *Registry of Deeds, Dublin, Abstracts of Wills*, 3 vols (Stationery Office: Dublin 1956).

ffolliott, R. (ed.), 'The 1821 Census Returns for the Parishes of Aglish and Portnascully, Co. Kilkenny' in *The Irish Ancestor*, vol. VIII, no. 2, 1976.

ffolliott, R., 'Irish Social Customs of Genealogical Importance' in *The Irish Ancestor*, vol. X , no. l, pp. 18-23.

Fox-Davies, A. C., *Heraldry Explained* (David and Charles: Newton Abbot 1971).

Froggatt, P., 'The Census of Ireland 1812-15' in *Irish Historical Studies*, vol. 14, 1964-5.

General Alphabetical Index to the Townlands and Towns, Parishes and Baronies of Ireland, Based on the Census of Ireland for the Year 1851 (Genealogical Publishing Co. Inc.: Baltimore 1984).

Hayes, R. J., *Manuscript Sources for the History of Irish Civilization*, 11 vols (G.K. Hall & Co: Boston 1965).

Hayes, R. J., *Sources for the History of Irish Civilization, Articles in Irish Periodicals* (G.K. Hall & Co: Boston 1970).

Henchion, R.,'The Gravestone Inscriptions of Co. Cork' in *Journal of the Cork Historical and Archaeological Society*, Jan.-Dec. 1967, vol. LXII, and Jan.-Jun. 1968, vol. LXIII.

Heraldic Artists, *Handbook on Irish Genealogy* (Heraldic Artists: Dublin 1980).

Herries, G. L. and Mollan, R. C. (eds), *Richard Griffith 1784-1878* (Royal Dublin Society: Dublin 1980).

Hussey de Burgh, U. H., *The Landowners of Ireland* (Hodges, Foster and Figgis: Dublin 1878).

International Encyclopaedia of the Social Sciences (The Macmillan Co. and the Free Press: 1968).

Johnson, J. H., 'The Irish Tithe Composition Applotment Books as a Geographical Source' in *Irish Geography*, vol. 3, 1954-8.

Johnston, E. M., *Ireland in the Eighteenth Century* (Gill and Macmillan: Dublin 1974).

Kidd, C. and Williamson, D. (eds), *Debrett's Peerage and Baronetage* (Debrett's Peerage Ltd. Macmillan: 1985).

Kuper, A. and J. (eds), *The Social Science Encyclopaedia* (Routledge and Kegan Paul: London, Boston and Henley 1985).

Leader, M., 'The Irish Parish Registers' in *The Irish Genealogist*, July 1957, vol. 3, no. 2.

Lewis, S., *A Topographical Index of Ireland*, 2 vols (London 1837).

Lucey, M., 'Rateable Valuation in Ireland' in *Administration*, Spring 1964, vol. 12, no. 1.

Lyons, F. S. L., *Ireland Since the Famine* (Fontana: London 1973).

Mackenzie, R. A., *The Time Trap* (AMACOM: New York 1972).

MacLysaght, E., *Irish Families: Their Names, Arms and Origins* (Allen Figgis and Co. Ltd: Dublin 1957).

MacLysaght, E. (ed.), *The Kenmare Manuscripts* (Stationery Office: Dublin 1942).

MacLysaght, E., 'Seventeenth Century Hearth Money Rolls' in *Analecta Hibernica*, No. 24.

Matthews, C. M., *Your Family History* (Lutterworth Press: Guildford and London 1976).

Mitchell, B., *A New Genealogical Atlas of Ireland* (Genealogical Publishing Co. Inc.: Baltimore 1986).

Mitchell, B., *A Guide to Irish Parish Registers* (Genealogical Publishing Co. Inc.: Baltimore 1988).

Nolan, W., *Tracing the Past* (Geography Publications: Dublin 1982).

O'Brien, R. B., 'The Story of the Tithes' in *Irish Ecclesiastical Record*, vol. 27, 1910.

O'Brien, G., 'The New Poor Law in Pre-Famine Ireland' in *Irish*

Economic and Social History, vol. 12, 1985.

O'Cinneide, S., 'The Development of the Home Assistance Service' in *Administration*, vol. 17, no. 3 , 1969.

O'Dwyer, R., *Who Were My Ancestors? Genealogy (Family Trees) of the Eyeries Parish, Castletownbere, Co. Cork, Ireland* (Stevens Publishing Co: Astoria, Ill., USA 1976).

Otway-Ruthven, J., *A History of Medieval Ireland* (Ernest Benn Ltd: London 1968).

Phair, P. B., 'Guide to the Registry of Deeds' in *Analecta Hibernica*, no. 23.

Phillimore, W. P. W., *Index to Irish Wills* (London 1912).

Pine, L. G. (ed.), *Burke's Landed Gentry in Ireland*, 4th Edition (Burke's Peerage Ltd: 1958).

Pine, L. G., *Your Family Tree* (Herbert Jenkins: London 1962).

Ryan, J. G., *Irish Records: Sources for Family and Local History* (Ancestry Publishing: Salt Lake City 1988).

Simington, R. C., 'The Tithe Composition Applotment Books', in *Analecta Hibernica*, no. 10, 1941.

Townsend, P. (ed.), *Burke's Genealogical and Heraldic History of the Peerage, Baronetage and Knightage* (Burke's Peerage Ltd: London 1967).

Vaughan, W. E. and Fitzpatrick, A. J. (eds), *Irish Historical Statistics* (Royal Irish Academy: Dublin 1976).

White, R. H., 'Rateable Valuation', in *Public Administration in Ireland*, vol. 3, 1954.

Williamson, D., *Debrett's Presidents of the United States of America* (Webb and Bower 1989).

Wood, H., 'The Destruction of the Public Record Office' in *Studies*, vol. II, 1961-2, pp. 363-8.

Wood, H., 'The Tragedy of the Irish Public Records', in *The Irish Genealogist*, vol. l, no. 3, 1937-42. pp. 67-71.